Carved into the ~~~~~ ~~ ~~~~~~~ ~~ ~~ *enigmatic and legendary sound engineer who was affectionately known in the music industry as "Little Buddha." Loved by musicians and producers for his mysterious and uncanny knack to produce hit after hit record, Little Buddha's identity has remained a virtual secret until now as Preston Nichols comes forward and reveals his hidden role in the recording industry. Already famous for his involvement in time experiments known as the Montauk Project and heralded as one of the few people in the world who understand the true physics of time, Preston Nichols explains how subliminals and mind control were used to influence the masses who listened to rock 'n roll.*

In The Music of Time, Preston integrates his extensive *knowledge of music with his insights into time and offers a new view of history and the universe. But, most chilling of all are his real life adventures. These include efforts by mysterious sources which enable Preston to parlay his resources into the ownership of different radio stations and enable him to set up his own facility for time travel research. At the same time, the hand of evil reaches into the equation and seeks to arrest Preston. Saved by a message from the future, he escapes that fate but cannot save his close colleague, John Ford, who is incarcerated without a trial and shipped off to a sanitarium for challenging the most politically powerful man on Long Island.*

The Music of Time is an intriguing look at the unknown *history of the music business which leads to a human rights saga that will make patriotic Americans cringe. Told against the backdrop of time travel, a new millennium begins to unfold.*

Cover Art:

Artist's depiction of the creation of the cosmos through the vibration of sound as represented by spirals emanating from a tuning fork

THE MUSIC OF TIME

By Preston B. Nichols
with Peter Moon

SkyBooks

NEW YORK

The Music of Time
Copyright © 2000 by Preston B. Nichols and Peter Moon
First printing, June 2000

Cover art and illustration by Ariel Phoenix
Typography by Creative Circle Inc.
Published by: Sky Books
              Box 769
              Westbury, New York 11590
              email: skybooks@yahoo.com
              website: www.time-travel.com/skybooks

Printed and bound in the United States of America. All rights reserved. No part of this book may be reproduced in any form or by any electronic or mechanical means including information storage and retrieval systems without permission in writing from the publisher, except by a reviewer, who may quote brief passages in a review.

DISCLAIMER The nature of this book necessitates clear statements of what is and what is not being purported. This story is based upon the memory, recollections and experiences of Preston Nichols. He has recounted these events to the best of his ability. It is up to the reader to evaluate their relative truth. The publisher does not assume responsibility for inaccuracies that may have resulted from induced trauma or misconceptions. Some names and locations have been withheld or changed to protect the privacy of those concerned. Lastly, nothing in this book should be interpreted to be an attack on the United States Government. The publisher and the authors believe and fully support the United States Government as set forth by the U.S. Constitution. Any heinous activities described herein are considered to by perpetrated by individuals who were not acting within the legal bounds of the law.

Library of Congress Cataloging-in-Publication Data

Nichols, Preston B. / Moon, Peter
    The Music of Time
by Preston B. Nichols with Peter Moon
      244 pages, illustrated
        ISBN 0-9678162-0-3
1. Time Travel 2. Music 3. Mind Control
Library of Congress Catalog Card Number 00-131453

This book is dedicated to John Ford and to all of the musicians and listeners who were unwittingly used

ACKNOWLEDGEMENTS

Jimmy Abbatiello
Greg Arcuri
Alexandra Bruce
Jerry Camisi
Dr. John Clark
"The Colonel"
Vince Glasser
Debbie Holton
Dr. Louise Mallory
Mary Ann Martini
Bob Nichols
John Quinn
Elena Sabella
Ronnie Vostinak

CONTENTS

INTRODUCTION • 11

PART ONE • 21

ONE • My Start in the Music Business   23

TWO • The Wall of Sound   29

THREE • Buddah Records   35

FOUR • Days of Future Passed   43

FIVE • Back to Brookhaven   47

SIX • The Lost Chord   53

SEVEN • The Physics of Music   55

EIGHT • Sex, Drugs & Rock 'n Roll   61

NINE • Jim Morrison   71

TEN • Special Effects   75

ELEVEN • Earthquake   85

TWELVE • Mind Control   89

THIRTEEN • Star Wars   101

FOURTEEN • Sky High   107

FIFTEEN • The Mind Amplifier   113

SIXTEEN •	Shifting Realities	125
SEVENTEEN •	Swan Lake	137
EIGHTEEN •	Victory at Sea	147
NINETEEN •	Science Fiction	153
TWENTY •	Pyramid Rock & the Laser Disk	157
TWENTY-ONE •	Espionage & Theft	159
PART TWO • 165		
TWENTY-TWO •	The Radio Business	167
TWENTY-THREE •	John Ford Arrested	175
TWENTY-FOUR •	The Air Force	183
TWENTY-FIVE •	Declared Incompetent	187
TWENTY-SIX •	Powell Destroyed	189
TWENTY-SEVEN •	Considerations	195
TWENTY-EIGHT •	The Future	201
EPILOGUE • 211		
INDEX • 225		

Also by Preston Nichols with/and Peter Moon

The Montauk Project: Experiments in Time

Montauk Revisited: Adventures in Synchronicity

Pyramids of Montauk: Explorations in Consciousness

Encounter in the Pleiades: An Inside Look at UFOs

by Peter Moon

The Black Sun: Montauk's Nazi-Tibetan Connection

by Stewart Swerdlow
Edited by Peter Moon

Montauk: The Alien Connection

The Healer's Handbook: A Journey Into Hyperspace

BY PETER MOON

INTRODUCTION

Throughout the last decade, Preston Nichols has developed a considerable reputation for his alleged involvement in time travel and secret government projects. However, it is not very well known at all that he was just as deeply involved in the music scene of the 1960's as rock 'n roll came to center stage in world pop culture.

Although I have acted as Preston's ghostwriter and co-researcher for a number of years, it was his expertise in sound engineering that brought me to meet him in the first place. This is very curious to me because I grew up with an antipathy to the subject. As I kid, I never understood what all the fuss was about when it came to stereo sound as opposed to monaural. It seemed to me that people were spending far too much time discerning the quality of sound rather than just listening to the music. I could detect a difference, but I always thought the music being played was far more important than the sound system it was played on. Therefore, I tended to tune out when someone would start talking about the virtue of one stereo system over another. That was until, one day, I heard about quadraphonic stereo. All of a sudden, my ears perked up. I wanted to know everything about it. I was even surprised at my own interest in the subject. I was not a technical buff, but I wanted to know about each track and each speaker and what all of the functions were. Unfortunately for my interests at the time, quad stereo in the late 1970's was nothing but a flash in the pan. Before I could begin to seriously think about buying a system, the fad was gone and written off as a complete failure, never to return to the commercial market since. In retrospect, there was only one significant aspect with regard to my capricious interest in a subject I had shown no previous interest in. It proved to be a premonition of my future and eventual collaboration with Preston Nichols.

In 1990, it had been over a decade since I had heard about quadraphonic sound. It was the last thing on my mind when I learned about another device that had elements of quad sound. At least, it had four speaker-like boxes and played music. It was owned by a chiropractor in Manhattan and was purported to balance the electromagnetic field that surrounds the human body. It was called the *Betar* and was put together by a man named Peter Kelly. A patient of the chiropractor told me about the machine and told me that a public company was being created to market it. The *Betar* was going to retail to the public for $70,000 a unit but would also be marketed to the medical and healing community. They were going to need a full brochure. As I was in the field of advertising and design, this patient thought that maybe I could help them. This interested me as a potential business proposition, and I felt that I had a good angle as I knew I understood much more than most advertisers do when it comes to esoteric aspects about the human body. I pursued the lead.

Eventually, I met the chiropractor in Manhattan. He showed me the *Betar* but complained that it was not set up right when he received it. It needed adjustments, and he had to make them himself. I did not know what he was talking about, but the device was aesthetically pleasing in its construction, and I just scoped it out. It had a reclining platform with four speaker-like boxes surrounding it so

INTRODUCTION

that while you rested comfortably, musical sound penetrated your energetic field. Two of the boxes were actually speakers and were directed at the center of the body. Two other boxes were opposite the other boxes and were input devices. The speakers sent waves directed at the body which bounced off and went into the input device. The doctor explained that this was a biofeedback device. He gave me a pair of goggles which he said would reflect my state of being at the time I was looking at them. I would see colors and patterns that my own biological system was generating as I listened to the music. As I listened to the music, the colors were a cross between a kaleidoscope and what you might see looking under a microscope, but they were always moving. After forty-five minutes, the doctor came over and brought me back to the real world. I was completely relaxed. What was particularly significant to me was that I remained relaxed for the entire day, even after a train ride from Manhattan to Long Island. Riding the Long Island Railroad has never been a pleasant experience for me. It has always been somewhat stressful, so this was a very welcome surprise.

Nothing ever came of the public offering for the *Betar*, but one day I was talking to a guy named Jeff who was studying to be a chiropractor. I was telling him about the *Betar*, and he said that he had been on it, too. In fact, he said there was an even better machine. It was put together by an inventor named Preston Nichols, and he said that I should check it out. Jeff said that Preston was not so much into marketing, but maybe I could help him. The device, he said, was about $60,000 cheaper. Another one of Jeff's friends was Margo Geiger, a nice older lady who worked as my proofreader up until her death. She told me that I must go to the Long Island Psychotronics

Association and listen to Preston. She said it would be absolutely fascinating.

I met Preston soon after but never got a chance to ask him about his inventions. He was lecturing with others and talked on and on about the Philadelphia Experiment and the Montauk Project. I was subjected to an earful of science-fiction-like information that I deemed the best story-telling that I had ever heard. It was all about time travel with a stunning array of technical oriented information. His stories also included the subjects of mind control, aliens, and Nazis who were allegedly operating an activity right under our noses on Long Island. Even if his stories were untrue, they were worthy of an "A" for creativity and holding one's interest. As it turned out, my life would be changed forever by the remarkable stories I heard that night. I met Preston to see if I could help him market his equipment but ended up marketing his incredible stories. Since then, writing and researching the history, legends, and circumstances surrounding Montauk has become an entire career.

When I finally got the opportunity to sit down with Preston and talk about his machine, he told me that he was the one who had invented the prototype for Peter Kelly's machine. He said that his own system did not have the goggles which he called "blinky lights." Preston did not advocate the use of these as they tend to be hypnotic and can be used to entrain a person's thought patterns to their detriment. Preston also told me that when the original quadraphonic systems were introduced, the people behind them did not really know what they were doing. He could show me a far superior system. It was not a quad system in the same sense that the sound industry had already produced. There were four boxes, but two of them were

INTRODUCTION

input devices, not speakers. The idea behind both stereo and quad stereo was to reproduce the actual experience of listening to live performers. His system, he explained, did that better than any other system on the market. After all, he had been in sound engineering since its emergence in the 1960's. He called his device the *Biofiss*. I will defer the technical description of that device to Preston, and you will read about it later on in this book.

Preston's music system was very much a focal point of his research into the paranormal, but as I interviewed him in order to write the *The Montauk Project: Experiments in Time*, he never really linked the subject of music to Montauk. Nevertheless, I heard many stories about his experiences in the music business and his work with different artists. These anecdotes were told to me in bits and pieces throughout the years. *The Montauk Project* book was basically a summary of a decade worth of research by Preston. It consisted of scuttlebutt he had heard throughout his years in the defense industry, countless interviews conducted at Montauk, as well as research done with people involved in the project.

The Montauk Project itself was put together as a result of human behavioral studies conducted secretly under the umbrella of Brookhaven Laboratories. These studies were done as a result of the Philadelphia Experiment in 1943 when the Navy experimented with degaussing technology and sought to make a ship, the *U.S.S. Eldridge*, appear invisible to radar. The Navy denies this, but the subject matter is still highly classified and considered to be the forerunner of today's stealth technology. Not only was the *U.S.S. Eldridge* reported to have become invisible, but the sailors involved were hurled out of this dimension. Upon their return, some were imbedded in the bulkheads and other fixtures of the ship with others spontaneously combusting or suffering severe psychological trauma. Even if one does not accept the more sensational aspects of the Philadelphia Experiment, there is absolutely no doubt about the fact that the sailors were exposed to non-ordinary electromagnetic fields as a result of the degaussing coils that were employed to demagnetize the hull. In order to first prevent negative effects on human beings, a massive study was eventually begun after the war, at Brookhaven Laboratories, in order to understand how human beings and the human consciousness relate to different electromagnetic fields. This research project also had at its disposal human behavioral studies conducted by the Nazis. Many of them were quite gruesome, but they were empirical in nature and were as meticulous as only Germans can be. They provided considerable information about human reactions.

It is no small irony that when Brookhaven Laboratories was erected in 1946, the location selected was Yaphank, home to the largest concentration of Nazis outside of Germany. Before the war, Yaphank sported an "Adolf Hitler Boulevard" with other streets named after Goebbels, Göring and the like. Many people of German descent worked at the lab as well, and there have always been questions about their loyalties. Not only did Brookhaven entertain top international scientists, many of whom were German, but it became the premier atomic and scientific research center in the world. Shortly thereafter, the National Security Act was passed and the C.I.A. was brought into being. Covert connections between the Nazis and the U.S. were completely affirmed when Allen Dulles, the first director of the C.I.A., hired Reinhard Gehlen to set up the working procedures of the C.I.A. Gehlen had

INTRODUCTION

served as the director of Nazi intelligence in Europe. Dulles also hired Ewen Cameron, the head of the American Psychiatric Association, to conduct mind control experiments under a program known as MK-ULTRA. These are documented facts, and no one who honestly researches this subject will deny it.

As the human mind was studied, and sometimes quite brutally, all sorts of empirical observations were made. Just as the Nazis had their own occult bureau and researched the supernatural, so did the researchers at Brookhaven. Finally, after years of research, there were successes in integrating the human mind with computers. The experiments in mind control, although limited, were successful. Eventually, this clandestine research was considered to be potentially very dangerous and the funding was denied. Nevertheless, great strides had been made in terms of technology and secret forces carried forward, eventually moving the project to a decommissioned Air Force Station at Montauk, New York. It was there that eye witnesses say that the research reached its apex on August 12, 1983, when a full scale hook up was made to the *U.S.S. Eldridge* in 1943 and time travel became a reality. The general pattern of this research is related in *The Montauk Project: Experiments in Time*.

Preston Nichols remembers entering the fold of the Montauk research when he became a paid employee of Brookhaven Labs in the late 1960's. But, his first recollections occurred when he was having a family dinner that included his cousin and her husband. The husband mentioned that he had seen Preston at Montauk, yet Preston had no recollection of ever having been there. This resulted in a heated argument. Over the years, more people began to recognize Preston from Montauk and other associations he had no conscious memory of. Preston soon realized that he had an entire life he knew nothing about. Memories were buried, including what appeared to be memories of other realities which were elusive but nevertheless tangible in many respects. All of these experiences fostered Preston's research which resulted in the book *The Montauk Project*.

This pattern of unrecovered memories is a primary reason why the music aspect of the Montauk Project was never dealt with in the earlier books. The connection was never completely made. He remembered being in the music business, and I knew something about it, but the working components of it and how it related to Montauk were overlooked by both of us. There was also another factor. Although I had suggested for years to Preston that he should do a book about his music experiences, he was always reluctant. He said he had angered enough people with *The Montauk Project*, and he thought this music book might be even more aggravating to certain folks. Consequently, he has not relayed many anecdotes at all about various musicians and their bizarre behavior. Nevertheless, there was key information he was willing to release that will hopefully serve as a springboard to further research and understanding.

Working with Preston on this book was not an easy task. For example, he gave me four separate times (about seven years apart) for when he first met his boyhood friend, Mark Hamill. Finally, I asked his dad, Bob Nichols, if he remembered Mark. Bob remembered Mark raking leaves in their backyard as a youngster. By going over different information from different angles, we were able to arrive at as accurate a representation as possible. Preston explained his disparities by telling me that he

INTRODUCTION

seems to live on at least three different time lines, and they get confused. He has appreciated this attempt to put his history into words because it straightens out his own memories

Preston is a genius. He is unsurpassed when it comes to understanding electromagnetic functions and all of the technical details that go with it. This is verifiable in science and industry and also makes him an irritant to those who would want to dismiss him as a mere crackpot or nut. He is also knowledgeable in psychology, religion and occultism and sees realms that regular human beings are cut off from. In esoteric terms, Preston occupies nonlinear space. This means that he is operating in a consciousness that is not regulated by linear thought. Therefore, his memories and experiences do not always conform to linear applications. This book is an attempt, and certainly not a perfect one, to put his experiences into a linear reality.

There are many controversial statements herein. I have made reasonable attempts to verify certain information, but these are Preston's memories, not mine. I can neither prove nor disprove certain statements. Also, his experiences often defy ordinary attempts to verify them. For example, false identities are common throughout his experiences at Montauk. Sometimes, people appear to be one person when they are really another. Preston Nichols was definitely in the music business as a key player and knew plenty of famous people. Whatever the truth is, it is always stranger than fiction. After you have read the entire book, I will offer some additional perspective on the relative truth of the situation.

The second half of this book takes us on another adventure all together. It concerns some of Preston's key activities post Montauk and attempts to harass and attack him that ultimately ended in the indefinite incarceration of one of his associates, John Ford, the founder and president of the Long Island UFO Network. What happens here is based upon cold hard documented facts that were chronicled in the local newspaper. It is an exposition of human rights violations, and a massive effort to hide the truth.

If the future contains endless possibilities, including a time when the truth of the universe will be fully known and the consciousness of man can move fluidly through time, there will be many stepping stones of realization along the way. This book and the stories herein are not a step back to the "The Land Time Forgot" but rather to the "The Land Where Time Remembered."

PART ONE

CHAPTER ONE

1

MY START IN THE MUSIC BUSINESS

My involvement in the music world goes back to 1958 when my father and I were deeply involved in scouting. One evening, while attending a "Blue and Gold Dinner" for Webelo scouts at Oscar's Bowling Alley in East Islip, the public address system suddenly went dead. We had been listening to a live band known as "The Recorders." I thought they were fantastic and so did all most everyone else. No one knew what to do about the busted sound system until the pack master told the band that one of his Cub Scouts could probably fix it. They got a charge out of that and said "Sure, let's see if the kid can fix it."

That kid was me. I took a look at the amplifier and found out it had a burned out resistor. I bridged it with some aluminum foil and this turned out to be an excellent temporary solution. The amplifier was working again, and the band continued to play. During a break in the music, I talked to the guys in the group and convinced them to let me do a demo tape of their music. My father then took me down to St. Mary's Church in East Islip where we borrowed their big Ampex tape recorder. We took it back to the bowling alley and did a demo tape of a song called "I've Had It".

The leader of the Webelo scouts from Bayshore was Cal Mann, a small time record producer and an aspiring performer. He thought the recording was great and played it for a friend of his who had just started his own label. This man liked the song, too, but he needed a better recording than what I had provided. He eventually called the Recorders up to Belough Instruments in Manhasset for a more conventional recording, but the sound was faulty. Finally, they had to get me out of grade school to get the recording they wanted. The record "I've Had It" was subsequently cut at Grand Award of Pickering and Company in Freeport, New York and was released under the label "Time Records." It can be found in CD format to this day. The name of the group "The Recorders" was changed to "The Bell Notes."

Cal Mann, the scout leader and record producer, had noticed my acumen in the area of recording. When I ran into him again during a camping weekend, he talked to me about his interest in music and told me that he was originally from Philadelphia. He was trying to break into the music scene in New York City.

One Saturday, Cal and I got together and talked for most of the entire day. At the time, he was renting a house that was filled with all sorts of old audio equipment which would be considered antiques by today's standards. Even in those days, most of what he had was considered to be old for the time period we were in. Based upon our discussion and what he had already witnessed with my recording of "I've Had It," Cal recognized that I was a whiz in electronics. He offered me four dollars an hour to work as his

MY START IN THE MUSIC BUSINESS

recording engineer in the hopes that I could do something with his old equipment and get his music career to take off. To a twelve year old kid at that time, his offer was huge money. I accepted it and told my parents that I had a job with a black fellow in Bayshore. When my mother saw his big limousine, she figured that he must be all right.

One of Cal's old audio pieces soon came in very handy for both of us. It was a "brush development corporation sound-mirror" and was patterned after the German ferograph, a recording device which came to this country after World War II. It had a cork capstan and was used to produce a hit song entitled "The Twist", a hit record which topped the charts in the early 1960's. Although I knew this man as Cal Mann, most of you will recognize him by his stage name of Chubby Checker.

When we took our taped recording of "The Twist" to Crest Records, they put it on their Ampex 350 but could not get the speed right whatsoever. Consequently, we had to trudge the sound-mirror down to Crest. When we played it on the sound mirror and put it on the 350, the audio engineer was curious about this piece of equipment and wanted to know where we got it. Cal told him that he had found it in the attic of the house he was renting. There were also some preamps and mixers in his collection which took me about three days to fix. This was accomplished primarily by changing the capacitors. Once I got everything to work, including the sound-mirror, "The Twist" did not sound too bad, as long as the speed was right. God only knows what speed that sound-mirror ran at as they did not have a standard in those days. It depended on how big the piece of cork on the capstan was. The capstan literally had a piece of cork wrapped around it and still does to this day. I know as I actually own the machine.

THE MUSIC OF TIME

For those of you who are too young to remember, "The Twist" was a huge fad and started a new trend in pop music. It is the only record other than "White Christmas" to reach number one on the charts two different times. One reason it caught on as a fad has to do with a very esoteric principle in sound recording. In fact, it has been a closely guarded secret until now, but we will go into that in detail later on in this book.

Although I had proven to be a success in the recording business, I still had to attend school. By the age of sixteen, I met up with a group of guys who became known as "The Ventures" and did a few of their albums. While working for them, I met up with Frankie Valle and the Four Seasons and eventually recorded them at St. Mary's Church in East Islip. Sometimes, I even used to fill in on the drums for them. If you listen to the song "Big Girls Don't Cry," you will hear me in the background. At the end of the song, you can hear my voice exactly, singing "Big Girls Don't Cry."

My early work with the Four Seasons taught me what I considered to be a very valuable lesson. Frankie Valli's real name was Frank Valenti and when his songs were released, the records contained the words "written by Frank Valenti." Of course, he lived under that name and could be easily found. Consequently, he was besieged by fans and ended up moving to New Jersey. I took this to heart and insisted that my name never be put on any recordings, even if only listed as sound engineer. That is why you will not see my name in too many places.

The general public does not realize how contrived some aspects of the music business really are. A prime example is Chubby Checker himself. If you consult the internet, you might find a web site that says his real name

MY START IN THE MUSIC BUSINESS

is "Ernest Evans". This is possibly going to cause people to say that I am making up what I am saying. If one looks at the particular web site I am referring to, it says that "Ernest Evans" is the "name" that was contracted to Cameo Parkway and was later changed to "Chubby Checker". It is not necessarily the true name of Chubby Checker. The man I knew referred to himself as Cal Mann, and he was the Chubby Checker who has become a part of pop culture.

As you read this book, there will be other discrepancies between my experiences and what publicity people write about music stars. In the music business, publicity is designed to cultivate an image that will sell records and make the person well thought of. There is also a deeper side to some celebrities and that includes mind control. Sometimes there are even stand-ins or doubles. The world of celebrity can be very convoluted. I know because I was right in the middle of it for many years.

THE MUSIC OF TIME

CHAPTER TWO

2

THE WALL OF SOUND

After getting involved with Chubby Checker, my career began to blossom. I became heavily involved at his company which was known as Parkway Records. Parkway subsequently bought Cameo and became known as Cameo Parkway. At the age of twelve, I was probably the youngest recording engineer in the field. As I continued my part time career in the record business, I was still growing up in East Islip. At the age of sixteen, I combined forces with a group of friends in the neighborhood. They provided the musical writing and performance, and I worked as their sound engineer. Although this group had considerable talent, we could not sell the music we produced to anybody.

It was during this period with the band that I met one of the most beautiful girls I have ever known. Her name was Lucy, and she was the cousin of one of my friends in the group. Lucy's two brothers hung out with their cousin, and I decided to make friends with them in order to meet their sister. These two brothers were Chuck and Mark Hamill, two people who were to figure prominently later on in my music career. Lucy and I did become very close friends, but she had already dedicated her life to God and eventually joined a convent and has since lived her life as a nun.

Despite the disappointment with Lucy and the neighborhood band, I still had a very active life and career in the music business. Nevertheless, I attended school and kept up with my studies. When I graduated from high school, my mother wanted me go to college. I not only thought that was a good idea, but I was also interested in studying psychiatry. My interest in the subject was no different than most students who study psychiatry or psychology: they want to figure themselves out. My mother was in seventh heaven because she was an art teacher with a psychology background and now I was going to follow in her footsteps. I attended Stony Brook University on Long Island. This was great for her until I came home one day and told her the subjects were not being approached properly. My language was not so diplomatic.

Although the subjects of psychiatry and psychology have made some progress over the years, they basically work on a paradigm of statistical analysis. In other words, they are trying to tell you that the mind of man can be statistically analyzed. The quantum model of the human mind is now beginning to come into psychiatry, but most of it is statistical and that is garbage. I soon realized that I did not want to study psychiatry.

I had now blown a year studying a subject I would not get a degree in. Consequently, I transferred to Suffolk County Community College and decided to study a subject that was already quite familiar to me: electronics. This was fun and relatively easy for me, but I decided I needed to get back in business and make some money. I spoke to one of my professors, Mr. Mayer, and told him I needed some work. He asked me what I could do, and I informed him that I had worked off and on in the recording industry for years, recording the Four Seasons out at St. Mary's Church as well as Chubby Checker and other local groups. Mr. Mayer said he had some contacts at Columbia Records and set me up for a meeting in Westchester at some sort of research facility for CBS Records.

I met with Mr. Mayer's contacts. They were very nice, but they said they had no place for me. One of the guys said he knew someone who had just purchased an old NBC studio on West 57th Street in Manhattan and wanted to rebuild it. I was told to go to the building and ask for Phil. He might be able to use me. I was not given his last name. When I arrived at the address and asked for Phil, this freaky looking fellow came out with a hairdo that extended out all over the place. He said, "Hi, I'm Phil."

I told him that I was Preston Nichols, a friend of Charlie from CBS.

"Oh, Charlie, how's he doing?" Phil asked. "I haven't seen him in such a while."

After we spoke for a while, Phil looked at me and said, "Why are you here?"

"Charlie said you needed someone with technical skills to rebuild some of your studio," I responded.

"Oh, yes, we do. We've got no money to pay for it though."

I told Phil we could make an arrangement. He claimed he could pay me $5 an hour. This was not horrible money in those days and was certainly well above average for a college kid, but it was not great either. Asking what else he could give me, Phil said he could hook me up with record producing and that sort of thing. I took the job and began working for Phil. His full name is Phil Spector, arguably the most famous and heralded record producer in the music business. Most of his success as a producer was in the early 1960's, but he also worked with the Beatles in their later years at Apple Records.

I began my work for Phil in Studio A on 57th Street. It was the oldest, dumpiest studio in the place. They had equipment in there from the time of Woodrow Wilson. But, it had an echo chamber, a real echo chamber. This was the famous Phil Spector "Wall of Sound" which many of you have heard of and all of you have actually heard through the radio at one time or another. It was a very reflective echo chamber. If you would clap into it, about fifty claps came back at you. On one wall in the back, he had six big speaker cabinets. He also had a group of microphones set up in the chamber. First, he would have the performer record the regular music tracks in the standard studio. Then, he would play the tapes into Western Electric amplifiers which drove these big old Western Electric drivers in the back of the echo chamber. The performer then sang in front of the microphone as everything reverberated. That wall of speakers was the Phil Spector "Wall of Sound".

Although this might sound glamorous, I can tell you that this was no dream job. The place was a mess, and it seemed every damned capacitor in the system was leaking and making noises. We called these strange noises "anti-artifacts". It was my job to literally rebuild Studio A and the system in the echo chamber. One day, I saw Phil standing nearby and asked him what standards he wanted this studio built to.

"I don't care. Do whatever you feel like."

That was all he said so I did whatever I felt like. I spent about three months, part time, building this facility.

THE WALL OF SOUND

Finally, it was beautiful and brand new. Phil called in his engineers and said to go in and have fun with it. When they went in, the engineers looked around at the equipment and said they had no idea how to run it. They said the kid he had hired (meaning me) had done some very strange things. Nevertheless, Studio A was the state-of-the-art recording studio for Phil's company which was known as Bell Sound East. There was also a Bell Sound in Los Angeles and one in Memphis. Phil owned all three and all were very popular, but Bell Sound East was best and became the Mecca for the best recording artists in the industry. What I did in New York was eventually copied in Los Angeles and Memphis.

When the top rock bands came in to do a recording, their producers and audio men would ask Phil for his best studio. He would refer them to Studio A, his newly rebuilt studio, but would also tell them that there was only one engineer who could operate it. That was me. They typically viewed me as a young kid cleaning the tape heads. When they asked about my qualifications as a sound engineer, they were informed that I had literally built the studio. Obviously, if I had built the studio, I must know how to operate it. In fact, I was the only one who could. In this way, I became the technical czar of Bell Sound and got to work with more famous recording acts than you could imagine. These included the Rolling Stones, Beatles, Beach Boys, BeeGees, the Mamas and the Papas, Jim Morrison and too many more to mention.

Although no one consciously realized it at the time, when Phil Spector gave me carte blanche to build a studio, he created a circumstance that would leave a lasting impression on the recording industry as well as all of humanity itself.

THE MUSIC OF TIME

3

BUDDAH RECORDS

Although I had given up my formal study of psychiatry, I still had a profound interest in psychology and what made the mind work. As I worked at Phil Spector's studio in Manhattan and studied electronics at Suffolk Community College, I was also doing experiments at Long Island University in the area of ESP. They had an open forum with all sorts of independent study programs.

It was during this time period that one of my friends in the neighborhood band said his cousin would be very interested in my ESP research. This cousin turned out to be Mark Hamill who I was already familiar with as described earlier. At that time, Mark was a member of a recording group called the "Ohio Express." He volunteered for some of my experiments and we hit it off and became friends. He had a very deep interest in the occult, metaphysics, ESP and all types of psychic phenomena. Originally, he lived in Ohio and would visit his family on Long Island. When he did, we would get together and discuss all sorts of different subjects. I tried to develop his ESP. We pooled our information and sought out many different types of occultism. Mark was extremely mystical. He consulted astrologers and was always looking for patterns in numbers and names.

Mark was not only a metaphysician, he was a gifted and prolific lyricist. He was an extremely talented musician as well and eventually starred on Broadway as Mozart in *Amadeus*. One of the reasons he was chosen for the role was that his musicianship was flawless. He also had the petulant personality that fit the role of Mozart exactly. He could basically be himself. Although he was offered the role for the movie, he turned it down. Perhaps he did not realize what a big hit it would become or did not want to be typecast in the role. I do not really know what his reasons were, but I saw his performance at least two times and it was excellent.

Before I got to know Mark very well, I was already acquainted with his older brother Chuck, an even more gifted musician. Chuck had been hanging around the studio for some time because he wanted to break into the music business. He had always demonstrated a great interest in electronics, audio systems and weird technology. Chuck was more of a technician than Mark and was down-to-earth. Sometimes he thought his brother was a complete idiot with his head in the clouds. I helped Chuck understand his brother, and I think I kept them in a decent brother relationship. There were times when he would have abandoned Mark had I not stepped in.

Chuck was also very interested in time travel and used to talk to me about it. He asked me if I knew anything about time travel technology or making a time machine. Whenever this subject came up, I could only joke about it. He took it quite seriously and said I would be the one making a time machine for the private sector in the future. When I asked him how he knew this, all he said was that

BUDDAH RECORDS

"he had seen it." If I did not know him better at the time, I would have thought that he was just one of the kids in the neighborhood trying to wind up the "scientific nerd" (meaning me) in the community to see what he could get him going on. This was not the case however because he had tremendous respect for my technical abilities. After all, I was the one who made his recordings work. Since those early years, I have also spoken to quite a few people who believe Chuck to be a time traveller. He was always interested in cutting-edge technology and eventually became very involved in the intelligence community.

As I became involved with the Hamills, I began to record their music. I had access to Studio A and Chuck was already familiar with the studio set-up from hanging around. The first record I produced for them was "Beg, Borrow and Steal" which was released by Cameo in October 1967 under the name "Ohio Express." Even though this record made the charts, it did not bring us instant success.

Chuck was not only a genius with electronics and music, he also had an acumen for business. One day, he said, "Let's make our own (recording) label."

"Sure," I said. "Why not? Everything else we've done is ludicrous. Let's try and make a label too."

After deciding to create our own company, the group of us sat around the kitchen table and brainstormed over what we were going to call our new record label. About this time, a young seven-year-old kid came into the room and looked around. Seeing me sitting about in a lotus position, which is the way I used to sit, he suddenly and unexpectedly blurted out "Mr. Buddha!" We all thought that "Buddha" was a great label name and decided to use it. One of the guys saw to the registration of the name, and we began to record songs under the name and spelling of "Buddah". Once we actually had a label, I was able to use all of my contacts at Columbia, Atlantic and elsewhere to get proper distribution. Although things started to happen, we soon discovered that none of us knew the record business all that well. I basically knew how to record and that was about as far as our expertise went. Consequently, we hired a man by the name of Neil Bogart to run the company. He claimed to be the nephew of Humphrey Bogart and certainly had a fascination with him. After my involvement with him, he renovated the entire first floor of his music publishing business to look like the night club set in the movie *Casablanca*. In our operation, he contributed about $250,000 to get Buddah off the ground. He became the president and owned about forty-eight percent of the stock. Another group of us owned the remainder. The company began to do well under his leadership.

A lot of the recordings we did for Buddah were performed and recorded with direct participation by the Hamill brothers. Many times, they would simply arrange the music and whip a band into shape so the recording would work. If the band was not up to snuff, they would work with studio musicians in order to produce a decent sounding recording. As a sound engineer, I used them liberally because they knew their music and were consummate professionals. Not all of the work we did together was released under the Buddah label. As an engineer at Bell Sound, I recorded all different types of groups. Sometimes, I would utilize the Hamills for the work I did under Phil. Other times, we recorded at Bell Sound for our own interests.

In Chapter One, I mentioned that publicity accounts of rock stars are not always accurate. A prime example of this can be found in the book *Rock On: The Illustrated Encyclopedia of Rock N' Roll: The Modern Years: 1964-Present (Volume II)*. If you look under the group with the name "Ohio Express," you will discover that Mark is not listed as one of the members. However, if you read further, it will tell you that Neil Bogart, one of the executives of Cameo, became affiliated with Buddah Records and took the name "Ohio Express," as well as his association with the producers, to release "bubble gum" music, the kind that had worked so well for the "1910 Fruitgum Company." This listing in *Rock On* also states that as the records of the Ohio Express became major best sellers, the "above lineup of musicians" were recruited to make personal appearances as the Ohio Express. This book is stating that the listed members of the band were for touring purposes only. This was very typical. Names were bought and sold all the time. The producers referred to above were myself and the Hamills.

The 1910 Fruitgum Company was also a result of my association with the Hamills. The book *Rock On* even lists "Mark" as the keyboard and rhythm guitar player for this group but gives no last name for him. It further states that the recordings were made by studio musicians and featured the lead voice of "writer-producer Joey Levine." This was one of Mark's pen names, taken from Joe E. Levine, the producer of the movie *The Ten Commandments*. Again, the listing in *Rock On* tells us that as the records began selling in the millions, a touring group was organized to make personal appearances. The first hit by the 1910 Fruit Gum Company was "Simon Says." It was bubble gum music aimed at youth and was composed by Mark and Chuck. Mark wrote the lyrics and gave credit for them to my mother because he remembered her teaching

THE MUSIC OF TIME

MARK HAMILL

This is a photograph of Mark Hamill from the album cover of "Goody Goody Drops" by the 1910 Fruitgum Company. He is listed as "Mark" with no last name although his name has been mistakenly transposed with that of "Rusty Oppenheimer."

BUDDAH RECORDS

CHUCK HAMILL
This is the man I knew and recognized as Chuck Hamill.
It is also from the album "Goody Goody Gum Drops" where he is
identified as "Chuck Travis," a pen name. I also knew him to use
the names Peter Knight, Gary Puckett, and Scott McKenzie.

him a similar song as his kindergarten teacher. The fidelity on that particular recording was phenomenal, and it is still equally good today in CD format.

The above involvement by the Hamills is corroborated by the book *Rock On*, but other involvements may be a little more controversial because popular "documentation" in the way of publicity books might not show it. These include Chuck Hamill singing the song "San Francisco (Be Sure to Wear Flowers in Your Hair)" which was credited to Scott McKenzie and became the top hit song during the Summer of Love (1967). Chuck also penned and performed songs in the studio for Gary Puckett and the Union Gap. They outsold every other rock group for the year 1969, including the Beatles.

There were many other identities these friends of mine assumed to produce hit records along with myself. They always wanted to keep their personal lives very private nor did they have the time to do all the touring that was requested as a result of their music. Together, we were trying to build a successful company at Buddah. As the hits began to roll out of Buddah and Bell Sound, I became known as "Little Buddah." I logged about two thousand hours of studio time and about two hundred of the songs I engineered made it to the top forty. That is a very good rate. It became "the thing" to make a recording at Bell Sound East with "Little Buddah."

Buddah Records did well under Bogart's leadership until we bought Kamasutra. That turned out to be a mistake. After buying another company, Plantation Records, we realized we had to get out of the record business altogether. But, that was many years later. There was still plenty of recording and excitement to be had in the music world.

CHAPTER FOUR

4

DAYS OF FUTURE PASSED

While attending college and also working at Bell Sound, my friend Chuck attended Juilliard, a prestigious musical conservatory in New York City. Looking back, I believe something strange happened to him there. One reason for this is that Peter Moon had some people do some research at Juilliard to find out if he attended the school. After looking for Chuck under different names that he has used, there was no record of him even having been at Juilliard in any capacity. I definitely remember him attending but also telling me that he became associated there with the Skull and Cross Bones society, a group that is more commonly associated with Yale University.

Chuck was apparently set up as some sort of CIA operative who was slated to work out of England. His father was already in military intelligence so the connection probably came from that quarter. Musicians are generally considered to be very good agents because they are innocuous and fade into the background. They come and go through different countries throughout the world and the governments never think anything of it. He ended up working at the London Philharmonic, and I believe it was the CIA who got him that assignment. They did not have to pull too many strings either because Chuck was a genius. You could give him a new instrument that he had never touched, and in a few hours, he would be able to play it as a virtuoso.

As Chuck worked with the Philharmonic, he also became affiliated with E.M.I., the primary music company in Great Britain. They recorded the Beatles and almost every significant group that came out of England.

The Beatles themselves had been connected with Phil Spector from their early days. If you have a chance to see the films clips of the Beatles arriving in New York for the first time, you will see Phil getting off the plane with them. Popular literature suggests that their first drug experiences were with him. Although I did not do drugs myself, they were very prevalent in the music industry and their factor with regard to mind control should not be discounted.

I became associated with the Beatles through my connection with Phil Spector at Bell Sound, a studio they utilized as it was the best money could buy. If you notice their early recordings, they are of poor quality compared to their later days. All of this changed with their album *Sgt. Pepper's Lonely Heart's Club Band* which has been hailed as the most revolutionary rock album of all time. Whatever its merits, it inarguably changed the direction of rock 'n roll. I was actually a participating witness to certain events which brought this new type of art form into being.

Most people will be surprised to learn that *Sgt. Pepper* was done by the Beatles as an answer to the then unreleased recording known as *Days of Future Passed* by the Moody Blues. All of the great rock groups were very

DAYS OF FUTURE PASSED

competitive. They listened to each others' recordings with appreciation but also with the idea of incorporating what they could learn for use in their own work. The Beatles were no exception, and as the most hailed and successful rock band in history, it stands to reason that they were at one time the most competitive. My memories of how they utilized the Moody Blues are as follows.

The original Moody Blues style was from the famous song "Go Now". That was their signature song and music style until Justin Hayward joined the group. I became acquainted with him during my days at Bell Sound in New York. At that time, there was a British fellow who used to hang around the studio a lot, and we played around with a lot of innovative technology and recordings. His name was Alan Parsons, and we were friends for years. He subsequently became famous as the leading member of "The Alan Parsons Project". Alan was also very strong friends with Justin Hayward and brought him to the Bell Sound studio.

The Moody Blues, mainly Hayward, wanted to do something symphonic, so I introduced him to the Hamill brothers. Chuck Hamill was the classical musician and Mark was the lyricist. They sold them a concept and wrote up a story to music entitled "Days of Future Passed". At that time, as Chuck was working with the London Philharmonic, they were able to get sections of the orchestra over to the studio. That is how we did "Days of Future Passed." At that point, Paul McCartney was hanging around with Phil Spector at Bell Sound and heard some of the musical rushes being played in the control room as the mix down was being done. McCartney liked it and subsequently came up with the concept for *Sgt. Pepper's Lonely Heart's Club Band*. I was brought in to help with certain sound effects. Almost every book claims that the sound was done exclusively at Abbey Road, but this is just not true. They did not have a proper facility at that time.

If you see a copy of *Days of Future Passed*, you will see that Peter Knight is the conductor of the London Festival Orchestra. This is actually Chuck as the conductor with members of the London Philharmonic in the orchestra. According to my friend and journalist, John Quinn, Peter Knight was interviewed in *Rolling Stone* magazine several years ago and talked about being on the run from the CIA. From what I heard, something went wrong with one of his operations and he became sought after himself. I do not know exactly what went wrong, but he never talked about it. In the early nineties, I would see him at hamfests from time to time and he would visit. He was always moving clandestinely and feared for his life. I have not seen or heard from him for many years now.

Here we had a mysterious genius who believed himself to be a time traveller and also thought that I would build a time machine myself. With his brother, he had conceived a record album that not only made major waves in the music industry, it was based on the theme of time travel with the words "Days of Future Passed." To this day, I still do not know what all these strange connections add up to, but it all has a lot to do with becoming more conscious of the principles of time itself.

CHAPTER FIVE

5

BACK TO BROOKHAVEN

One day, I was doing a recording session for the Rolling Stones. I forget what recording we were doing, but I believe it was *Jumping Jack Flash*. Mick Jagger suddenly walked into the control room and said he wanted to talk to "Little Buddah" and see all of my recording equipment. He knew of my reputation as a recording engineer and considered me a fountain of good ideas. He said that every time I worked for the group, he learned something new. He usually knew what sound he wanted, and it was my job to produce it. On that day, he wanted to learn what secrets I had to share. Subsequently, I took him home so that he could see what I had. He talked a lot about the occult and procedures of sexual magick. He often used these techniques before recording.

As things developed, I decided it would be a good idea to introduce Mick to the acoustics of the old Montauk Pavilion. It was called Caswell's Pavilion and was at Caswell's Beach, not too far from Dick Cavett's house and the future home of Mark Hamill. We got permission to use the pavilion in order to record a couple of songs for one of the Stones' albums. Both of the songs, "You Don't

Always Get What You Want" and "Street Fighting Man," utilized a choir of young boys from Montauk who showed up at the pavilion and sang. I have no idea where they came from. Mick became enchanted with Montauk during this period and began to live there for long stretches of time. To this day, his picture can still be found in certain bars around the town. He expressed part of his affiliation with Montauk in a song entitled "Memory Motel" which is the exact name of a motel on the main street in town. An interesting anecdote about the Memory Motel was told to me at a lecture by a woman from Montauk who said she suspected that "Room #1" of the motel was a secret entrance to the underground. She had seen military personnel there and said the room always had something weird associated with it. As I recall, this was the room just to the north side of the bar. I told her that I had tried to rent that room several times but was always refused.

I really do not know if Mick Jagger had any direct connection to the Montauk Project. My memories of him were of a regular and routine nature although his interest in the occult and his strong attraction to Montauk and the Memory Motel will cause everyone, including myself, to wonder. His song "Sympathy for the Devil" is supposed to refer to Aleister Crowley. He has also produced low budget videos which explore satanism.

What is interesting about this time period is that I had begun to work at Brookhaven Labs during my summer vacation from college. This was in 1968. As an engineer and scientist, I had signed up for a program whereby I could work with their particle accelerator. There were several other budding scientists who were similarly interested. This was a paid job, and I was sold a bill of goods that I was doing something very patriotic for the good of my country. Unfortunately for myself, I was not assigned to the particle accelerator work as I had hoped. Instead, they put me on human factor research. I was to set up electromagnetic fields of certain types and subject actual human beings to them. Behavioral scientists, including myself, would record the stress and reactions of the test subjects. Looking back, this was research carried forward from the original Philadelphia Experiment. I was being used on some level by characters and factors I knew very little about.

As my work at Brookhaven occurred during my heyday at Bell Sound, I believe they hired me so that I could put thought forms on the recordings I was doing in the rock world. I do remember literally encoding thought forms into the music in what can best be called an "electromagnetic telepathy" of subtle energies.

As the recordings were being transferred to the tapes, I concentrated on the heads of the tape recorder in order to place a thought form on the tapes. If you want to encode a thought form, all you have to do is listen to the music that is being copied and concentrate on the playback machine heavily. By "grooving along" on the music but also concentrating on the thought form, you get a parametric impression on that tape of the thought form. We put thought forms into the music mainly to make people respond. At the recording studio, I literally compressed thought forms that people responded to in particular ways. One of the most simple thought forms projected were to make certain rock groups popular. We simply put a thought form on the recording that you would want to hear it again. Once you heard the song over a transistor radio, the thought form would go out to "buy the record and play it over and over again until it was worn out." Then, you would go out and buy another record. That is how come we sold so many records.

In Chapter One, I alluded to "The Twist" being popular due to a very esoteric principle in sound recording. There are actually two thought inputs into a sound system when a recording is made. This includes what could be termed the "psychic input" of the musicians as well as that of the performer. When the performer stands in front of the microphone and sings, he projects a thought form into the coil or the capacitative element of that microphone. That capacitative element (the capacitor), basically consists of electronic plates with an insulator designed for the purpose of storing electrical potentials which can be reproduced at a distant point, such as a speaker. There is also an amplification process which amplifies the wave forms and eventually creates loud music at the receipt point (the audience).

Sound waves are part of the electromagnetic spectrum. It is the electromagnetic function which is the key. Thought forms also make their own impingement on the electromagnetic background of the universe. For example, if you hear sound waves telling you there is a sale at a department store, you have also acquired the thought form that the managers of the store wanted you to have. Sound waves themselves are generally much more easily measurable and discernible than those wave forms produced by thought forms. In other words, the electromagnetic functions of thought forms are much more subtle and is indeed an esoteric subject in itself. But, all of you can easily perceive how thought forms are carried by sound waves when you consider the prospect of hearing something you don't believe. For example, suppose you hear a politician say something. Inside of you, you can perceive that he is not telling the truth. It is not necessarily the sound itself which tips you off. The radio or sound system is actually projecting a duplication of what emanated from the origination point. You just "pick up on it". In actual fact, the thoughts you "picked up on" were the result of electromagnetic impulses. The telepathic wave forms are subtle (less dense) in comparison to what ordinary science would refer to as wave forms, but they are nevertheless present and can be monitored within the realm of the electromagnetic spectrum. As I said earlier, it is an esoteric science. We will go more into the technical details of how this can occur in the physical spectrum, but first it will be necessary to go into some background theory on the metaphysics and physics of music itself.

THE MUSIC OF TIME

CHAPTER SIX

6

THE LOST CHORD

Many of you have heard of the Moody Blues' album entitled *In Search of the Lost Chord*. For those of you who have not, perhaps you have heard of this "lost chord" which is commonly referred to and pronounced as "om" or "ohm" in esoteric circles, particularly those of the eastern tradition. It is also known as the "monochord."

The lost chord refers to the perfect state of creation or that state of consciousness which existed before reality existed. The idea of expressing the word *om* is to reunite one with the supreme consciousness. *Om*, in its most perfect sense, represents the complete electromagnetic spectrum. That includes all of creation. When we consider the principles of hard physics, everything in creation falls within the realm of the electromagnetic spectrum. This includes all matter and energy, including light, sound and different types of matter. When we consider the lost chord, we are talking about what Lao Tzu called "the uncarved block." In other words, it is creation undisturbed by anything. In the Qabala, the first principle of creation is known as "The Fool" and it is represented by the Tarot card of the same name. The fool refers to a capricious or

THE MUSIC OF TIME

whimsical impression upon the inherent state of perfection and creates a break in the supreme state referred to as *om*. Ironically, the word "ohm" refers to a unit of electromagnetic resistance. In a general sense, this is analogous to what happens when "the fool" whimsically presses upon the lost chord. He has created a unit of electromagnetic interference. Actually, the foolish impulse has created a whole series of electromagnetic waves that conform to some whimsical principle. More impulses create more waves, including light, energy, and matter. Ultimately, you have an entire universe such as the one that we live in. The search for the lost chord refers to our attempt to regain the understanding of all of this.

When we contemplate these matters in a more practical sense, we are faced with another amazing irony or synchronicity when we consider E.M.I. Thorn, the electronics and music conglomerate which figures so enigmatically in the Montauk Project book series. The initials "E.M.I." stand for Electronic Musical Industries. At least, this is what the company's name is. But, in the field of electronics, "EMI" stands for "Electromagnetic Interference" and is in common English dictionaries as well. It is as if this company is somehow directly responsible for the electromagnetic interference which has taken us away from the lost chord and attaches us to this reality. If you then throw in the concept of "thorn," you have more esoteric significance. It refers to the thorn in the "Christ Consciousness," another name for the perfect state of creation.

The above is the metaphysical background of music, for all music derives from the above. Next, we will look at some of the principles of music from a more physical perspective.

CHAPTER SEVEN

7

THE PHYSICS OF MUSIC

As we examine the physical aspects of music, it is necessary to address the human factor and how the human mind interfaces with the entire scenario. The first step is to realize that our reality, or reference frame for consciousness, is based purely on sounds, notes, tones, or whatever you want to call them. All of these aspects are frequencies. In actual fact, every physical object or manifestation you can conceive of conforms to a frequency or can be identified as having a particular frequency. It is all frequency based.

Matter itself starts out as a wave traveling through space. Next, the wave hits a magnetic field. That magnetic field hits it, twists it and turns it into a particle. It is now matter. This immediately brings to mind an age old consideration of when does a particle become energy and when does energy become particle based, i.e. matter. This is best explained as the difference between "particle light" and "wave light."

When light is traveling in a vacuum, without a magnetic field, it's a wave. When it hits a magnetic field, that field will take the wave (or energy) and curve it. It spins the wave and makes a ball of energy that we call a particle. It is known as a photon. Based upon nothing else but the spin of the energy being spun into a particle, we can safely say that we are dealing with a frequency. When psychics talk of "vibes", they are referring to frequencies. A human mind, or human being for that matter, is composed (or at least situated with) many complex frequencies. We are all a very complex group of frequencies. The (electromagnetic) signature of a human being is a complex group of frequencies.

Our reality is actually a group of frequencies or an ensemble of notes. Intelligence, or lack thereof, is dependent upon how the frequencies relate to each other. Frequencies can be related in amplitude, cycles per second and phase. Amplitude signifies how strong the frequency is, i.e. how much power is behind it. In musical terms this would be loudness. Cycles per second is the tone. But, what is phase?

Phase, not frequency, is probably the most important concept when it comes to understanding the mind. Phase refers to the relationship of the starting point of one wave to another wave. For example, if you have one cycle starting at one point in time; then another begins five seconds later or five seconds before, that is phase. Phase is primarily concerned with timing. Let us say you have one cycle starting off at Point A. Phase would refer to another cycle starting at a slightly different time, before or after the preceding cycle. Phase can become very complicated because it can refer to the same frequency or multiple frequencies. When we are dealing with phase, there is an infinite variety of relationships that can be very difficult to understand. The role of phase is better understood when we consider thought forms.

THE PHYSICS OF MUSIC

What exactly is a thought form? It is a group of interrelated frequencies, including amplitude, phase and every other aspect one can measure. This is illustrated very well when we consider a piano where each key on the piano strikes two strings called a doublet. Although both strings are tightened to relatively the same degree, it is theoretically impossible for them to be exactly identical in tension. Therefore, two different frequencies sound out when they are struck by the hammer. Although they are almost the same for practical purposes, the difference would be undetectable to most human ears. The reason two strings are used is that the two separate offset frequencies (again, they are only very slightly offset) created a "single" sound of their own which is more harmonious than if you just heard one of the strings by itself.

The example with the piano is also referred to as a heterodyne effect. "Heterodyne" in the dictionary is defined as "designating or of the combination of two different radio frequencies to produce beats whose frequencies are equal to the sum or difference of the original frequencies." In esoteric or psychotronic lingo, a heterodyne refers to the fact that two or more frequencies make a sum which is entirely different than its respective parts. This is an excellent way to control the masses. By playing with certain frequencies you can induce riots or raucous behavior. Conversely, you can subdue a wild crowd by the same methods. Such manipulations were reportedly accomplished by black helicopters in Los Angeles during riots that were triggered as a result of the Rodney King verdict. The helicopters allegedly transmitted frequencies that induced peaceful behavior in the crowd. In New York, black helicopters were also observed but no significant damage occurred. Although there was plenty of rabble-rousing and protesting of the Rodney King verdict in Brooklyn and Harlem, the New York media helped any helicopter activity by judiciously conspiring with the police to play everything down. When skirmishes happened, they were not reported so as not to alarm the black population. Thus, no riots in New York.

Phase, to summate, consists of different frequencies (sometimes the differences are very subtle) which are offset but when grouped together develop into a creation of their own. This is often considered a thought form. This thought form can combine again with human thoughts or consciousness in any number of different manifestations.

Now, let us consider the human brain. What is the whole physical human system really all about when we consider the human mind? The model that was accepted in the government projects I was involved with is that the brain is basically a very smart interface to the "real mind." The real mind is multidimensional and its "headquarters" can be found in a parallel reality that is in a reference frame 90° away from this one. In dimensional terms, this can be thought of as the 90° relation between a line (one dimension) and a cross (two dimensions). An additional projection of 90° from the cross will give a third dimension.

When I refer to the human mind in terms of phase, it is offset by 90° from the brain. In science, if you say something is offset by 90°, it is considered to have zero value. This is illustrated in practical terms if you consider that two currents of voltage offset by 90° equate to no power. It does not exist in our reality. But, there is undeniably a connection between this brain and the mind. The mind is a group of frequencies which the brain represents in its frequencies, but our mind is actually 90° away from this reality, in a frame that has length, width

THE PHYSICS OF MUSIC

and no height. It is a two dimensional world. That is why most people do not think terribly effectively when you consider the wide panorama of intelligence and capability within the brain. They are not making contact to the rest of the dimensions. If they are only thinking in the reference frame 90° away from here, there are only two dimensional references. This is the mind-set of most of the population on Earth today.

The general population is beginning to rise in awareness, but there is a difference when we consider higher dimensions of existence and extraterrestrials. They think in three or more dimensions. Most humans think in only two dimensions because they are not aware of other reference frames away from the 90° point. One can also consider the proposition that spiritual beings inside of human bodies have been conditioned not to think in reference frames away from the typical 90° point. Theoretically, if you are thoroughly hooked up and your mind is totally constituted in all these other dimensions, it is continuous and integrated. It could also be said to be complete or "whole." This concept is the inspiration for the term "holy." To be "whole" is to be "holy". Therefore, if you connect the mind and all of its connections to the physical, you are whole.

The Montauk Project concerned itself with manipulating the way different sections of the mind communicate with different realities in different dimensions. In this manner, one can control what the mind is thinking and what the mind is doing (in this reality). The curative idea is that the more you can consciously get yourself into other dimensions, the more continuous you can be. Consequently, you would be less subject to anything in this three-dimensional reality. Obviously, the Montauk Project dealt with compartmentalization rather than integration. It is the opposite of what one considers "holy."

CHAPTER EIGHT

8

SEX, DRUGS & ROCK 'N ROLL

The esoteric aspects of the Montauk Project were very intricate. First, I will address how the human mind interfaces with all of it.

According to current knowledge, the Montauk Project is intimately tied to the creation of our reality or, at the very least, resonates with a project or activity that does so. As consciousness is the basis of reality, the activities at Montauk were designed to regulate consciousness, particularly the electromagnetic grid or matrix of thought forms that permeate and influence our culture. In this book, we are concerned with the latter with regard to the world of music and entertainment. More crudely, this has been termed "sex, drugs and rock 'n roll."

I have spoken about rock 'n roll, but what about drugs and sex? There were definitely drugs at Montauk. One proof of that is Timothy Leary, the famous or infamous (depending on your viewpoint) psychedelic guru. Witnesses from Montauk remember him passing out drugs at Camp Hero during the hippie period. This was during the early years of the Montauk Project. Anywhere you have

Leary, drugs are going to be a major factor. He was a very brilliant man in some respects but drove himself to dubious extremes with drugs. We also see evidence of drug experiments in some of the rooms at Camp Hero. If you look at my video tape, *The Montauk Tour*, you will see a room on the base with strange wallpaper patterns. There is a black and white room out there, too. Black and white stripes were painted all around the room with a white ceiling and a black floor. If you get a hold of Timothy Leary's second report on LSD, you will find it shows that exact type of room. In addition to the black and white room at Montauk, one was tiger striped, one room had psychedelic patterns, and another was painted with random colors that loosely looked like confetti.

Leary, who was associated with Harvard University, was initially hired by the CIA and military intelligence to develop conditioning drugs in order to make soldiers aggressive and that sort of thing. The aggression drug they use on soldiers today started with Timothy Leary. There were also experiments with truth serums, i.e. drugs that make people talk. The CIA and military intelligence has a vast drug section which Leary was heavily involved in.

Quite a few of the altered states used in the Montauk Project were drug induced. We had one drug — I do not really remember the name of it — which took about an hour to take effect, but when it did, it made you psychically wide open to the entire universe. Many people died from it because they could not take the experience. It is not easy to be that wide open. Unless you are prepared to be that open, your heart is going to stop from all the chaos. Next, the whole nervous structure becomes totally confused and your physical body shuts down. Many drugs were administered at Montauk, but I did not get involved with that nor

SEX, DRUGS & ROCK 'N ROLL

the taking of them. I was more of a radio, tube and antenna person, but I did get involved in programming people.

There is no question that there is a major connection between the drug world and the Montauk Project. This is highlighted by the fact that many locals know Montauk Point to be the major conduit of illegal drugs into the east coast to this day. This came to light when an attorney litigating a case against the East Hampton chief of police reported to Peter Moon that there are virtually no drug convictions for importing drugs in the entire area from Montauk to New Jersey. These "no convictions" are in stark contrast to a higher number on the rest of the east coast. Locals report that fires are set at night on the beach to signal drug laden boats where to come ashore. This is how the drugs are smuggled in. There is no serious enforcement with regard to cracking down on the illegal fires despite many complaints.

With regard to the music industry, drugs are well known to be rampant in that culture. Rock groups or stars are often kept high by key executives in a controlling and manipulative manner. This was particularly notorious during the years of the Montauk Project where many of the artists do not even remember what happened or when or where they recorded what song.

I have given a brief view of drugs but what about sex? Sexuality has been discussed at various times in the Montauk books, but to get down to the nitty-gritty, your psychic energy is basically your sexual energy. There is absolutely no difference. Sexual energy is your energy with your signature or your group of frequencies encoded on it and that is it. It is open energy or raw psychic energy. Whoever ran these various projects was very much enamored with sexual magick. The Montauk Project was literally loaded with sexual magick. It therefore behooves us to ask what exactly is meant by that term.

Sexual magick basically consists of taking your sexual energies and putting it into different channels within your being and doing things which could best be termed as "magical." It is well known in the orient that if your mind is continuous and whole, you can bring up the kundalini energy flow and do all sorts of amazing things. Kundalini is basically using the spinal system as a laser. You are bouncing the energy between your base chakra (which is at the end of your spine beneath your gonads) to the crown chakra (located at the top of your head). As you bounce the energy back and forth between the base and the crown, it amplifies with each bounce. It builds and builds until eventually you have a roaring monster in there if you do not know how to control it. Too many people end up in that unfortunate situation when they try to unleash these energies. At Montauk, methods were used to raise these energies to an astronomical figure, but it could not be left in the person. That would kill them. The technique was to tap it or access it and amplify it further. The Montauk Project was basically sexual magick amplified, amplified through ten to the 24th gain via a particle accelerator. I intend to discuss more about this in a future book tentatively planned to be called "The Time Travel Primer". This will discuss how to use an accelerator similar to a gyroscope to time travel as well as several other subjects concerning time.

As far as sexuality is concerned, it is the channel through which your entire psychic energy reverberates. I am not talking about sexual potency here but of the energy flows that take place in the body. If you take these energies and properly use them, you have probably got the most potent form of magick in the world if you know how to use it. This is what was done at Montauk. Sometimes, sexual magick was used to calm down reality. This embraced weather control, including hurricanes.

In term of music and mind control, the music that is of the greatest interest to controllers is that which creates the most response to the raw public. That is, of course, raw sexual music or rock 'n roll.

Rock 'n roll is basically a reproduction of the orgasmic cycle put to music. In this "orgasmic cycle," you have these groups and ensembles of music that just bounce back and forth. The heart rate speeds up and then synchronizes to the rate of the frequencies of the music. The spinal channel is also excited. All of this occurs through the art of music. If rock 'n roll was just the reproduction of an orgasm, it would be a simple and perhaps innocuous matter. The problem is that when the orgasmic channels open, the person is totally opened up psychically and is prone to suggestion on the deepest most archetypal levels. As mind control meets rock 'n roll, there is a "raw gut thought form" taking hold of the audience. The process begins with a thought form which is reproduced with audio tones or music.

When we consider what music really is, it is basically a thought form. If you have a movement in a symphony, that group of frequencies is representing a concept as a thought form. The music becomes a frequency transformer. When we further complicate music by putting together technologically synchronized music through an audio output, there is a whole new set of factors that show themselves. This can be described as a continuous running ensemble of audio frequency tones related by timing, related by frequency, related by phase, and related by

THE MUSIC OF TIME

amplitude. When the end result of the music is interfacing to a physical system like a human body, timing becomes important because the audio ensemble needs to synchronize to a nerve pulse that runs continuously.

Why?

The reason is that the nerve is acting as a carrier wave for the music or thought form which is acting as mind control. It is just like a common carrier wave in electronics where waves carry intelligent information such as audio for the radio or pictures for the television. In the application I am talking about, the entire nervous system can become a common carrier for pictures, audio and feelings. Those in engineering can better understand the nervous system in this regard if they consider it to be like a stochastic signal processing system. All of this has to do with a common concept in electronics which is called "pulse position."

In order to understand pulse position, it is necessary to first understand the term "synch pulse." A synch pulse is a pulse that continuously repeats in time. It is synchronous because you always know where it is. It is like a reference point. When there is another or additional pulse with respect to the synch pulse, you have the phenomenon known as "pulse position" which is designated by the relationship between the two separate pulses. The other pulse might be a millisecond away or more. The second pulse is a set time position away from the synch pulse.

While the above is ordinary basic electronics, the equation becomes very complicated when we consider pulse position with regard to human beings. Humans have an entirely different "synch pulse" in that their references are floating or changing all the time. To pin down this floating reference, one has to engage in fractal analysis and stochastic positioning of the different patterns that involve very advanced signal processing. The details are for hard core engineers only.

If you visualize the human body's neural system to contain a "synch pulse" or floating reference frame, you can understand that music can enter the system through the audio sensors and create a pulse position with regard to the human bio-energy field. Although the music itself could be the carrier of mind control transmissions, it is not always that simple. Modern audio systems can contain pulses that can tag along with the regular electronics of the music and carry coded information that has instructions all its own. The codes could be something simple like a binary code or a Morse code whereby one millisecond equals a zero and two milliseconds equals one. Or, it could be so complicated that it could only begin to be deciphered with a very fancy spectrum analyzer. The codes themselves would be designed to interface with the neural network of the human body.

Pulse position is actually how your nervous system works. There is a synch pulse that represents the normal human state. When other pulses enter the system, they represent different phenomena including human reactions. When we consider these "other pulses," one can literally take one neuron and put thousands of signals on it. The pulses themselves are transmitted through the neurons. Keep in mind that each neuron is not only transmitting the resonant "life beat" of the human being, which I earlier referred to as the synch pulse, but it is picking up all sorts of semi-random pulses that have to do with the organism interfacing with its environment. Some of these are pleasurable and some of them are painful. If you take an audio amplifier, connect it to a neuron and turn up the gain, you will hear a sound that is like static or white noise. You would actually be listening to semi-random pulses and each pulse that comes through is a click. If you can then locate the synchronizing pulse and decode the pulse position, intelligent information can be retrieved. This is the same way audio or video signals, which are considered intelligent information, are decoded in regular electronics. All of this is why the start and stop of different notes in music is so important: because it translates to a multiple pulse position system. In other words, different notes or combinations thereof, resonate with different parts of our physical and mental structure. Consequently, the sounds can be pleasing or aggravating, depending upon how they synchronize with the activity that is already present in the neural-net.

Remember, what you hear is going to every part of the mind because your mind is a common carrier. So while some part of the mind is going to find it very enjoyable, another part of it is going to find it revolting. I have had people sit and listen to particular recordings and watched different parts of their body tense up and relax. Observing their physical body reactions demonstrates that one is dealing with a common carrier system. Someone gets excited while listening to music because it is interfacing into the neural-net activity of their body in different ways.

If you take your stereo and turn it up loud, you can begin to entrain another person. The neural-net is using only so many differentiated pulses with its floating "synch-pulse." When loud music begins to generate many more multiple pulse positions than the neural-net is accustomed to, it creates an overload. The idea in mind control is to jam the neural-net and stop it from its normal functioning. Loud music in itself can do that, but it can also be used, quite deviously, to lay in coded messages. Wacky or fringe people often spout out that they are receiving coded messages through the television or radio. The further study of this phenomena might reveal that some of these wacky claims might have some basis in fact.

Entrainment by music can also be witnessed in indigenous tribal rituals or even New Age drumming circles. If drumming is loud enough, you will feel it and your body will become entrained. For example, it is a scientific fact that a normal heart beats at about seventy beats a minute. If a drummer beats at eighty beats a minute, what is going to happen? The heart rate is going to rise to eighty beats a minute, too. If you do not believe me, you can try it yourself. If you drop to a nice and slow beat, after a while, it will have a hypnotizing effect and slow your heart rate down. This is the whole idea of using music as a method of mood control. It also shows how sensitive the neural-network is to music.

In this chapter, I have given an overall view of how sex, drugs, and rock 'n roll combine to make excellent tools for mind control. In the next chapter, I will discuss my involvement with one of the key performers from this period who to this day is still considered a "god" to his legion of fans.

THE MUSIC OF TIME

CHAPTER NINE

9

JIM MORRISON

I met Jim Morrison and the Doors about three days before the session where they recorded "Light My Fire." We met at a diner in Manhattan and struck up an immediate friendship and became pretty good friends. The Doors were a California band and did most of their demo tapes at Bell Sound West. Eventually, it got to a point where most of their recordings were being done at Bell Sound East. I was hired as a sound engineer by Bruce Botnick, a fellow who had a contract with Warner-Elektra, a company who rented the Bell Sound studios. Consequently, you will see that many of the credits on the Doors' recordings go to the Botnick Company and not to myself. As I have said elsewhere in this book, I never wanted groupie attention.

I arranged the sound for many of their songs and also groomed Morrison to be a better singer and performer. When he first started, he was reluctant to face the audience when he sang, especially a big crowd. He stood with his back to them and was very shy in public. He was not so shy in private. In fact, he liked to do recording sessions totally naked or with his shorts on. For some reason, he actually sang better in this state. We worked many hours to develop his style. In the beginning, he drank a little and that was about it. Drugs were not a major factor in the beginning of his career although they consumed him later on. As he performed more and more music, he went the drug route and became more and more stoned. It became my job to sober him up. I remember one particular time when we were recording the song "Touch Me." That is the song which features the words "I'm gonna love you 'til the heavens start to rain." We started out, and he was just awful. After awhile, I finally told the producer that I was going to take Jim across the street and fill him with coffee and milk. I brought him back to the studio in about two hours, and he was able to do the song. This was the stuff you had to put up with in order to work with him. The song "Touch Me" contained an imprint to make people feel good. Every so often, a song was entered into the repertoire of different groups to make people euphoric when they heard it. That was the song chosen for the Doors. It was done toward the end of their career when they were beginning to fade. That song, with its psychic overlay, is what kept them going a bit longer.

Jim Morrison has been celebrated as a very gifted poet, but it is unknown that he purchased a lot of poetry from Mark Hamill. I remember one of Mark's original poems was "Celebration of the Lizard" which I thought was pretty sick. Mark had hundreds or thousands of pages of lyrics laying around that he had written over the years. If someone wanted to buy some, he would hand over a whole stack and have them pick out what they wanted.

Morrison was also very interested in sexual magick as was his wife at the time who is also known as a Wiccan priestess. Although he tried to interest me in having some involvement with them in that regard, I never took him up on it. We were just very close friends. As Jim's involvement in drugs and alcohol became more severe, he would sometimes act crazy and become violent. I was the only one who could handle him at times and was often called over to assist in this regard. I am not sure why I was able to deal with him. He always claimed that he was part American Indian and said that the Indian side of him was the one who was either in control or out of control. He definitely recognized that I was part American Indian and that could be part of the bond that he and I had.

Most of the world believes Jim Morrison died in 1971. From an objective point of view, the coroner's report raised more questions that it answered, but I personally know that Morrison did not die. He took some combination of drugs and alcohol and became catatonic. He was more of a vegetable than a human being at that point. To the best of my knowledge, there was a meeting of producers who discussed what to do about their fallen rock star. Keep in mind, Morrison was viewed as a god in some circles. The producers reportedly came to a conclusion that his music would probably sell well if he had died as opposed to being confined to an institution. The best solution was to fake his death.

I know this to be true because I was called over to his house in the mid-1970's. He was in the Paramus, New Jersey area, and I was well into my study of ESP and psychic activity. I was sought out as an advisor to see if he could be reached by psychic means, and I came over with a number of mediums and the like. Morrison was quite fat by this time and would just sit in a chair and stare into the fireplace. Every so often, he started to come around but would soon revert to the catatonic state. As far as I know, he never recovered.

THE MUSIC OF TIME

CHAPTER TEN

10

SPECIAL EFFECTS

Besides Jim Morrison, I had the opportunity to work with all sorts of famous acts, but I was not interested in the hyperbola that is associated with that sort of thing. I was basically a sound engineer who happened to be very good at what I did and was sought out by different people for my professional services. In the process, I literally watched the recording industry find itself and made many contributions along the way, not only in sound engineering but in subliminals, too.

One of my biggest contributions to rock 'n roll was developing a deep heavy bass sound by basically making a twelve-inch speaker and putting it in front of the bass drum. Before I introduced that concept, in about 1963-64, rock 'n roll was not all that loud. It did not have that big of a bass sound. It was basically a person singing into a microphone with a small PA system and a couple of guitars each plugged into a 20 watt amplifier which used a pair of 6L6 vacuum tubes. This was still the vacuum tube era, and the Montauk/Brookhaven crowd loved their vacuum tubes because there was a lot of semi-black magic involved in the construction of them. But, in order to get the heavy bass sound, we coupled the bass guitars right off the speaker voice coils directly through attenuators and equalizers, or sound-shapers, right into the console. This resulted in a very deep, heavy resonant bass sound which changed the face of rock 'n roll.

In the 1960's, the studio practices were nothing fancy. The age of digital technology had not come in yet, and it was basically just microphones, tape recorders, and mixing boards. Special sound effects were created either through fuzz boxes, phase-shifters (which basically delays the sound or signal that goes through the circuit) or echo units. In those days, we did not have harmonizers, vocalizers or any of that stuff.

A typical recording session involved setting up microphones with either an eight-track or sixteen-track unit. Generally, each instrument was recorded onto a separate track. After this was a "mix-down" which consisted of processing all those tracks down to one or two, depending upon whether we were doing a mono or stereo production. In many cases, we did both because LPs were stereo, but 45s were mono and it does not sound good to take a two-channel stereo and mix it down to one. If you do, you get a lot of phase cancellations and it can sound like it is all in a barrel. Thus, in that era, the recording engineer was much more important because he literally made the sound that was put on the phonograph disc and eventually released. We literally had to "sculpt" the sound from the initial session tapes that were made. Many times, we had to take over a recording session and act as producer, arranger, and recording engineer because although the various groups had their own people, very few of them had any concept of how to make a "live" sound. They were not necessarily bad musicians, but to do

SPECIAL EFFECTS

a good job, you have duplicate what it feels like to be in front of a live performance with the band right in front of you and all the ambiance and charisma that goes with it. The "feeling" of the sound has to be canned into a microphone and eventually onto a vinyl disc. This is an art in itself and is why the recording engineer of the 1960's was as much of an artist as the performers were.

Most of your recording engineers had to have a very good working knowledge of music. I learned this from my mother, Virginia or "Ginny" Nichols, who was a fully qualified classical musician. Her primary instrument was the organ. She knew all of her music theory and passed it on to me as I grew up listening to all of the classical pieces on our RCA phonograph. Starting at about the age of six, I was given a good basic knowledge of classical music. All of the themes for the rock 'n roll pieces you hear today come out of or can be found in the classics. There are really no "new" musical themes on this planet. They have all been put down by Mozart, Beethoven, Tchaikovsky and others. After the great composers wrote down all of the musical themes, composing became a matter of rearranging and restating them and doing musical statements.

Besides the bass sound and the regular recording that I did, there were many special effects that I created in the music industry. This started with guitar sounds, and I also developed different fuzz boxes or distortion boxes. Although acoustical guitars have a great pure tone and sound beautiful, they are not at all suitable when you are trying to produce work that is in the category of "sex, drugs and rock 'n roll." To put it simply, this was raucous music, and the acoustical guitar did not quite hack it. Can you imagine Jimi Hendrix playing an acoustical guitar? When Hendrix and that crowd wanted to go with their loud sound, I got involved with developing bigger and louder amplifiers for the guys to make their raucous sound. It had to be raucous as well as loud. We would take a guitar with either an acoustical pick-up or a magnetic pick-up on it. Where the acoustical pick up is basically a microphone put inside the sound chamber of the guitar, the magnetic pick up is where the strings actually become a moving magnetic surface. As the strings change, the reluctance of the core structure of the coils and the magnetic structure creates wave forms or signatures. These signatures are based upon the vibration of strings and the intonations put on the vibration of the strings by the design of the structure and design of the body and neck of the guitar. It was an art form that was basically magic.

As each string vibrates, it changes the distribution of the magnetic fields and the pick-up. As you change the distribution in the magnetic fields of the pick-up, it then has lines of force cutting the coils which sit below the string in the electric guitar. It is the increasing and decreasing in strength of these coils that generates the wave form which translates to sound out of the amplifier.

I got heavily involved in distorting and shaping the sound of Hendrix's guitar. In fact, when Jimi was introducing that sound in the 1960's, most of that equipment had been personally built for him by myself. I also built the big amplifiers he plugged into when he played live. And, I can tell you, it was loud. It was blasting. He started out in the smaller clubs with his little practice amplifier that had a pair of 6V6 vacuum tubes in it that put out maybe 10 watts. He cranked the level up full blast and then played with the bass and treble and mid-range control to get the sound he wanted. We later evolved this system into a fairly complex group of pedals. As the musicians hit the

SPECIAL EFFECTS

different pedals, they could get almost any sound they wanted out of their guitar. All of these sounds had to be picked up and reproduced faithfully in the recording sessions. I got into designing all sorts of effect boxes or effect pedals. If you went to an early concert, you would have seen a guy playing a guitar with four or five pedals in front of him. He was switching things in and out, changing the levels, and changing the tone. The biggest thing, the Hendrix sound, was very simple. All we did in the old days was to take a ten watt vacuum tube amplifier and drive the thing all the way into a distortion. Turning it up as high as it could go, it came out with a semi-square wave with a raucous sound. I also had to design smaller units that could be put in between the guitar and the bigger amplifier because if you take a 250 watt amplifier and distort that, you will crack windows. Therefore, I had to design a little box so that the same sound could be reproduced with a more powerful amplifier.

Besides the guitars, I also became involved in choral arrangements. As I alluded to earlier, recording was pretty simple. Your compilations or chorusing was done by having the same person sing four or five different times into a multitrack tape recorder. When all the recording was done, you would then blend those tracks together so they sounded proper. This is another example of what is called mixing, taking 8, 16 or 24 tracks down to one or two tracks. Occasionally, it would be taken down to four tracks. Sometimes, one person would be singing, but it would sound like three or four singing with the same voice. First, the rhythm or musical accompaniment would be recorded. Next, the singer would put on headphones and listen to that track as he sang along. His entire sound would be recorded on another track. The singer would

THE MUSIC OF TIME

then listen to that track as he again sang along with it. He might do this three or four times, sounding better and better with each recording. This technique is how you get a nice rich vocal sound. This is not really enhancing the singer's ability to sing, but it is giving phase and time differentials within the main vocal so that it does not sound discordant. It makes the voice sound richer.

One of the more popular vocal groups I worked with were the Beach Boys. I originally met the Beach Boys when they came over to the east coast to do their recordings. Although the west coast had better publicity people, we had better studios. Contracts and publicity were often handled in California, but at that time, New York was the Mecca of rock recording and any group that was anybody did their recordings there, including the Beach Boys. Their first couple of songs, "Surfin' Safari" and "409" I believe, were done at Fox Studios in California because the father of Brian, Dennis and Carl Wilson was sort of a director at 20th Century Fox. Unfortunately, the movie studio equipment was not very good, and the only recordings they could produce were monaural. That is the reason why quite a few of their early songs were only recorded in monaural. When they got some serious money behind them, they recorded their songs in New York and worked with me. The Beach Boys were a nice bunch of guys and were easy to work with. Although they were easy going, they were always very concerned about the sound and wanted to know what every little thing sounded like. I fit right into their concerns because I was the one that basically created the final sound. I worked with their voice harmonies which I call choral rock. I was sometimes known as the chorus man and the bass man. We all learned from each other.

SPECIAL EFFECTS

There is an interesting story that my dad likes to tell. One day, he came home from a rock collecting trip to find a big truck backed into the back yard. He got out of his car, walked up to it and found a guy on the back of the truck playing an organ with the tail gate down. The organist told my father that he was playing with the guys in the back yard. When my father got to the backyard, my mother told him that these were the Beach Boys. She told him they had to stop over while they were doing a local concert so I could do some repair work on their amplifiers. As I busily worked in the garage, they made use of their time by practicing and attracted all sorts of people from the neighborhood who watched the free practice session.

The man playing the organ was Daryl Dragon, the son of Carmen Dragon, a famous orchestra conductor. Most of you will recognize Daryl Dragon as "The Captain" of "The Captain and Tenille" who were a popular act in the 1970's.

The Beach Boys were right in the midst of a general change of music in the period of 1967 to 1968. I call it a movement from "frying pan rock" to a more theatrical instrumental rock, of which the albums *Days of Future Passed* and *Sgt. Pepper* were prime examples. On albums like *Sgt. Pepper* with songs like "Day in the Life," we utilized different eight track machines and had about 100 different channels that were blended in to make those strange sounds. I was often asked to come up with a sound and inevitably did so for this album. These were the types of things a recording engineer had to do.

Some time after my sound work on the *Sgt. Pepper* album, McCartney and Lennon both liked what I did at Bell Sound. They approached me and asked me if I would be interested in building a studio in England. I told them

I did not want to go over to England and build a studio, but I did offer to build one here which could be transported and set up over there. They wanted the most modern studio possible. Bell Sound had a lot of vacuum tube technology, so I basically built them a solid-state studio. It was built in a warehouse on Long Island, tested here, and then flown over to England. I spent about a week at Abbey Road getting it together and working.

I also worked on creating the Melotron for the Moody Blues. This was put together by myself and two other friends. It was basically a bunch of eight-tracks played with a keyboard. There was one particular belt recorded on an eight-track system and you had a choice of eight tracks to play. The tape was either slowed down or speeded up when you played it. This created some very strange sounds. This was similar to what were known as "broadcast carts."

There were many other songs and effects I created or participated in. Many of you in the reading audience may remember a song called *Winchester Cathedral*. I did that with a megaphone directed straight into a microphone. I still have the megaphone in a closet somewhere.

One particular good sound effect I created was one with a thunderstorm in it. I had listened to all the thunderstorm tracks available and thought they stunk. I made it my business to go out on the roof of the building with a tarp, tape recorder and microphone and wait for a thunderstorm to come up. I made my recording of a thunderstorm and it was far superior to anything else ever heard. It can heard on the Doors' "Riders on the Storm."

There are countless stories and anecdotes, but the preceding information is just to give you the idea that I really was involved in the music business on a deep level.

SPECIAL EFFECTS

The accomplishments I have relayed here were primarily a professional matter. The next chapter concerns another special effect from sound engineering that reaches into the beginning realms of virtual reality.

THE MUSIC OF TIME

11

EARTHQUAKE

In the 1970's, somebody decided it was time to add some accent to the typical "disaster" movie and make the audience actually feel what was happening. The venue chosen for this was the film *Earthquake*. As I had quite a reputation in sound engineering by this time, I was brought in as a consultant to help the production company figure out the best way to create the phenomenon of an earthquake via sound technology.

The first thing I did was to bring the sound producer for the film over to the Dayton P. Brown company. There, I asked a friend of mine to run what is called a "shake table". This is actually a shake table transducer which looks like a huge bullet and is about two feet long and eight inches thick. Basically, it is a sound device which shakes. I had my friend run it at 10 hertz as we hooked it up to a flat bed device. It actually could displace a ten foot square of wood by about two inches. The sound producer was amazed and said it was the biggest speaker he had ever seen. I told him that we could make the entire floor of a theater shake if we used this same principle and the floor could be hooked up in the same way.

Actually, there were two methods to create the feeling of an earthquake. The shake table system was used primarily in premium, older theatres which had a wood floor as well as a cellar by which you could access the floor with a jack stand. The transducer was placed under the jack stand and hooked up to a huge amplifier. When a subsonic signal from the soundtrack was relayed, the shake table transducer would displace the floor about an inch each way. This became the preferred system for *Earthquake* and it became known as "Sensuround" or some name like that. It actually worked very well. As you sat in the theater and the earthquake started to sound off on the screen, the floor would shake. In fact, it worked so well that when we set it up in the old Huntington Shore Theater, it shook the building so much that all sorts of stuff fell off of the acoustical tiles on the ceiling. The manager of the theater called me up over this and said we had to turn the thing down. When I told him where the amplifier was and told him what to do, he called back in fifteen minutes and said he was not going to touch anything. There were too many signs saying "high voltage" all over the equipment. So, I had to drive up to the theater and turn the level down on the shake table amplifier which I had just that day brought into the cellar with a big forklift. Many times, the displacement of one or two inches shook the whole building of the theaters and the shake table was discarded.

Most theaters had cement slabs for floors and were not suitable for the shake table. If there was a cellar with an appropriate wood floor, the manager or owner of the theater had two options. He could either shake the floor or rent big speaker boxes that were placed in the auditorium and driven off of a 10,000 watt stadium amplifier. This was the second method of creating the feeling of an

EARTHQUAKE

earthquake. Instead of a subsonic signal to shake the floor, a supersonic signal drove the big stadium amp which drove the huge speakers. This made huge rumbles and it felt sort of like a thunder clap. These were actually air pressure blasts from the speaker cabinet.

Although I did not devise the second system, I did come up with the idea on how to implement it by encoding it on the magnetic sound stripes which run down the sides of ordinary celluloid film for making movies. In a simulated movie earthquake, the vibration you felt was the result of sound waves in the supersonic range which were encoded a sub-carrier on the magnetic stripes for the soundtrack (which was made up of four tracks). These were summed and put into a decoder that gave you an output for 30 hertz on down. In other words, the decoder read the supersonic carrier and put out ELF (extremely low frequency) signals. These drove either the shake table amp, when we were moving the floor, or the subsonic speaker amp for the huge speaker boxes in the theatres. These were so big that you could literally walk inside of them. They had about a dozen eighteen inch woofers in them. Each cabinet took in about 2,000 watts. The stadium amplifier was rented and put out about 10,000 watts. It had a range between 5 hertz and 20 kilohertz.

What created the earthquake sensation was the fact that 10 or 15 hertz was being amplified so that the wave was coming at you as an atmospheric front. The wave consisted of peaks and troughs with significant pressure differences. The audience was basically being shook with the wave front instead of the floor going up and down. Some theaters actually used both systems. While the pressure waves were hitting you, the floor was moving and making for a real dynamite effect.

This is a prime example of how sound waves can be used to create a remarkable special effect. Unfortunately, there are other sound effects which are considerably more subtle and quite sinister. We will explore them in the next chapter.

CHAPTER TWELVE

12

MIND CONTROL

During my days in rock 'n roll, the use of an echo was a big deal. The basic meat and potatoes of sound enhancement or sound reinforcement was the echo. There were many different types of echo devices, but the first ones to do echo effects were Les Paul and Mary Ford. This was back in the 1950's when the first group of tape recorders had three heads. There was an "erase head" to clean the tape, a "record head" upon which the recording was made, and a "play head" to play the recording. When a tape was in record mode, the play mode was not disabled because it was necessary to keep track of what was being laid down on the tape in case their was an imperfection in the sound. This also made it convenient for creating an echo effect because the two heads are an inch and a half apart which translates to about one-tenth of a second delay. If you take the output from the playback amplifier and feed it right back into the recording amplifier, it goes around and around and generates an echo. It is that simple.

There were many different types of echo devices. The most common one was described above. There were echoes recorded relating to both width and depth. There was a cacophony of different echo systems in the music industry. The one I used to get a kick out of was a big coiled garden hose. A speaker was placed at one end of the hose and a mike at the other. It sounded terrible but made an echo and was used. I built a system that had twenty-two different tracks of echo that were all blended together to make a very rich cacophony of sounds. Total harmonies of sound were created using echoes. I did these during my days with Phil Spector.

In order to "sculpt" the sound, one has to be familiar with the entire chain, all the way from the musicians' performance and what the microphone does to what the line amplifiers, echo decks, and coils do. Earlier, I said we were creating a piece of art. This could best be termed as a "painting of sound" which was what I used to call it. We were doing a sonic visualization of a concept in sound that the musicians were performing. It was very important to get this painting of sound to come through the little 45 RPM record player that RCA sold in those days. We had all sorts of equalizers and other sound-shaping equipment in the room as we mixed. Each record was treated as an experiment, but it had to meet certain standards. Did it sound good? Are the kids going to like this? It is not as simple as having the Beatles play in your living room, putting up a couple of microphones and making a master tape which is then recorded onto a phonograph cutter. If you do that, the sound will literally come out like trash.

In making records, we were usually not concerned with whether or not the sound from the musical performance to the audio speaker in the home was faithful to what the musical performance was. In business, the primary objective was to produce a sound that would appeal to the audience so that the record would sell.

MIND CONTROL

Typically, the live musical performance sounds nothing like the sound that comes out of a record player in the home. This is why I literally had to be an artist and shape the soundscape or presentation of each musical recording.

In the 1960's, most of the radio stations were AM, so we had to make sure that the recording also sounded good for that format. This required another whole chain of electronics that went from the radio station to your home. From the turntable in the radio station, which was a better quality turntable than anyone had at home, the sound had to go through the line amplifiers and mixer in the radio station and then to the transmitter. Once there, the sound was processed with peak limiting or over easy compression. These are technical procedures which make a radio station sound good to the public. Finally, the sound projected out of the little plastic radio on the table and made a noise that could be enjoyed. At the same time, we had to ensure the sound was something close to what came out of the 45 rpm record player. I now refer to it all as black magic because if I had to sit down and tell someone exactly how to do it, I could not. It is all too complex.

I picked up most of what I learned on my own. When I entered the music field in the early 1960's, there were no great recording engineers at that time. The ambition of recording engineers at that time was simply to reproduce the musical performance as best as possible. That was what RCA did with Elvis Presley. It is also why the Elvis sound, in so many cases, was clean and pure. There was no processing because he really sounded like that. Little Richard and Buddy Holly are two other artists who really sounded like their recordings. If you listen to any of the better recordings of these guys on a modern CD with a really good sound system, it sounds fantastic. It is as if they are right in the room with you. Of course, most performers were not in the category of the above artists. But, even if they were, producers soon learned that when an RCA record player was replicated by all sorts of other companies, as it was, there was no way one could predict how Elvis or anyone else would sound on a little 45 rpm record player. In the mid 1960's, the entire concept of record production changed. Producers realized that records could still be sold by the older methods, but the teenagers were getting more sophisticated. Therefore, we had to be very concerned with what the sound was that came out of the customers audio equipment when he played a record or tuned in to a radio station.

It did not take long to realize that there were other things going on in the recordings besides the electrical representation of the audio program we were putting on the tape. There were not only hidden agendas and procedures for increasing sales, there were more sinister things afoot. Today, I now realize that I was doing psychic overlays on the tapes. I found out that I could literally influence the way the sound was perceived at the other end of the audio chain by basically concentrating on the head stack as the tape went through it in record mode. I mentioned this previously, but now it will be discussed a bit more technically. This activity was the legacy which I had brought over from my association with Brookhaven and the Montauk Project. This was how the subliminals began.

There are two types of subliminals that were used in this time period. One was the psychic overlay just described. There were also true sonic subliminals. Many people will remember the Beatles' record where "Paul is Dead" was recorded 30 db below the chorus. There are other ways to do this as well. "Paul is dead" could also be recorded backwards in the chorus. Whatever method is used in the sonic route, it can be just as effective as the psychic overlay.

The music was basically formulated to be hypnotic and grab your attention and entrain the person listening. But, in the psychic overlay technique, I realized we could put in whole messages. Basically, I discovered that what I concentrated on as I ran the mix board and watched the tape going through the machine was just as important as what the sound actually sounded like at the other end. I finally got to a point where I had an interim step between the mix down and the final master. This consisted of me making a dub or a copy and concentrating on the recorder head as the copy was being made. That is where the psychic overlay was particularly successful.

When I explained this psychic overlay technique to Phil Spector, he said he did not believe me and wanted to see proof of it. Consequently, we set up an experiment. As we did the dub, I concentrated on a phone number. When the record was finally released, we got thousands of calls to that number. The message got through to people. The psychic overlay was impressed into the master tape and from there to the vinyl. When the record was played on the radio station or in the home, people got the idea to pick up the phone and dial this particular number. It should be pointed out that there was no phone number mentioned in the music. We were very careful to have a piece of music where there was no phone number in the lyrics or anywhere else. A special phone was set aside for the experiment, but he did not keep track of the individual calls.

After that experiment, Phil totally believed in concentrating on the tape. He wanted to use it for marketing purposes. Phil wanted us to put a thought out so that when you heard a song on the radio, you had to go buy it. I participated in these psychic overlays through about 1971.

The psychic overlay work began in 1968 when I first began to work for the Montauk/Brookhaven people. There are probably a multiplicity of reasons I was selected for this activity, but it likely had a lot to do with the fact I was doing hot tracks in the studio just about every other day, music that was destined to be heard on air waves across the world. To tell you the truth, I am not even sure myself about all the things they had me do. I was told something by the Montauk/Brookhaven people and would then overlay it for them. My own personal genius in the area of electronics and sound was, of course, at their disposal.

What I did was develop a "psychic overlay" system to the point where it was actually designed into the hardware as an electrical overlay. This was accomplished through an extra head that was placed on the opposite side of the tape than the regular head and was called the "cross-field head" or "cross-head." This received an input, via a vacuum tube audio amplifier, from a circular coil that was placed upon my head. As I created thought forms, this coil picked up slight magnetic emanations from my brain which are known as scalar waves. There were no real "words" transmitting from the amp to the extra head, only a quantum component (the scalar wave).

This innovation of a second head or "cross head" is exactly where the Aki corporation came up with their "cross-field bias". A bias is defined as a frequency which is above the audio spectrum (100-300 kz) which is mixed in with the audio signal being put into the record head in order to make the recording linear. If this is not done, a recording will sound extremely distorted. People from

Aki were in the recording studio one day and saw what I had done. They scratched their heads and wondered what the extra head was for. Eventually, they came up with their own idea, but they had no idea what its true function was. Their product was an abomination and served no useful purpose. It was just a "copycat" action.

In order to avoid any confusion for the reader, I will describe exactly what a bias is and how it functions so that a tape can register sound. The head on a regular tape recorder is basically a piece of magnetized metal, also known as an electromagnet. The reason you have a bias is because of the tape used in tape recording. A typical piece of plastic tape has inlaid upon it a bunch of tiny little pieces of iron or other metallic oxides. It is basically a metal powder. For practical purposes, we can consider these pieces of powder to be tiny little magnets which are confused and jumbled. Because they are disoriented, it can be considered a chaotic arrangement or a nonlinear function. What the bias does is create a geometric magnetization so that there is a cohesive or orderly pattern. We call this a linear function, but you would recognize it as something which makes sense. To be technical, the bias aligns the domains of the tape with the term *domain* referring to the way the magnetization arranges itself within the geometry of the tape.

The way this fits in for recording purposes is as follows. A performer creates a sound by reason of his/her voice or through use of an instrument. This generates an electric imprint or representation upon the diaphragm in a microphone which in turn makes an audio signal. The amplifier just amplifies the signal and makes it strong. The audio signal or signals are connected right to the coil in the head (there is actually a coil within the head) which magnetizes and demagnetizes the tape based upon the energy that is there at the exact moment when the head contacts the tape. As the tape moves across the head, it is magnetizing the tape at many different levels and many different polarities. When the magnetized tape moves along the "play head," the magnetic fluctuation from the tape generates electric current in the head which is a replica of the current that it took to record the tape. This is a very simplified version of how a tape recorder works. It is a somewhat detailed account of an ordinary function. There is nothing paranormal or unusual in this.

What is of particular interest in the above description is the chaotic function of the magnetic particles on the tape. I found that by concentrating on the record head, I could add to the imprint that was being put on the tape via the ordinary audio signals. Do not believe for a minute that scientists can account for every last particle on a piece of magnetic tape. This gets into the area of fractals and an analysis of the infinite. It is an open ended proposition that subliminals can be conveyed this way. I know it to be true based upon my own personal experience and that of others. Those who find this a bit of a stretch can consider an obnoxious commercial or song that repeats itself in your mind. What is the power of that sound so that it can impinge upon your consciousness to the point where it can haunt you, even for a very short time? There are numerous explanations as to why your mind could respond that way, but subliminal suggestion is a very plausible explanation for many such instances.

For me to concentrate on various recordings took quite a bit of time and energy. It was not too practical in terms of time management. The second head or "crossfield head," which I referred to earlier, was very useful in this respect. So that I did not have to concentrate full time, a tape loop of concentrated subliminals was made and looped through a tape recorder and put through to the extra head. This was another electronic means of "psychic overlay." It was often a standard audio program with somebody speaking subliminals into a mike. This tape would be recorded with both heads in use. The original head recorded the ordinary audio input. The second recorded the psychic input.

A typical recording system will have a range from 20 kilohertz to maybe 50 kilohertz. Some even get up to a megahertz, but most music recording does not require anything beyond that. What I had to do was make a system that would enable them to record at a frequency beyond the normal ranges that would be "hearable" to the mind but not within the ranges of ordinary human perception. The signal was there but would best be described as a hyperspatial factor. It could not be detected by ordinary means or measuring devices.

In the above situation, phase plays an important role. When the looped subliminal was then mixed in with the regular recording, the subliminal was fed into the system "out of phase", but the regular bias was "in phase." This worked extremely well, and I did not have to concentrate anymore. This means that the scalar wave was pressed onto the record, the phonograph cartridge picked it up, and the local sound system reproduced it. In fact, we also did the same phone number trick with this electronic means of the psychic subliminal. It worked very well, too. Of course, we never told anyone we were using subliminals at that point because they were illegal. It is still illegal, but the government never came across this method of doing subliminals. Therefore, they did not know of it so could not regulate it. If you consult pure physics theory as taught in universities, the field was cancelled out. Theoretically, this means that there is zero impregnation on the tape. It is immeasurable by routine methods. If it went to court, the judge would have to throw out the case because if he did not, they would all be admitting to paraphysics. Documenting it would present too many problems for the Federal Communications Commission.

Over the years, we developed a system which could literally put a thought on a phonograph record. You would not be aware of it consciously, and this was the method I believe they used to "tag" the Montauk Boys.* The subliminal thought might be "go visit this particular night spot on this date." Everyone that answered the subliminal and went to the spot was identified and placed on a list just because they had the sensitivities to pick up the signal.

This was also great for getting records sold. Just about any record could have significantly increased sales by using this method. Recently, I saw a friend of mine who ran into one of my old colleagues who commented how unusual it was that just about every other record I made was a top ten seller. He definitely believed I was doing something magical to get that kind of a result.

As there were so many different sound systems on the market, maybe 30 or 40 brands, obtaining a consistent sound was quite a problem. None of the systems sounded exactly alike. The point is that what actually sold the record was not so much the sound but the subliminal because it was the only thing that came through unscathed.

---

* The term "Montauk Boy" originated as a colloquial term used in my Montauk research to describe boys or young men who have received some sort of mind control programming via the Montauk Project or some similar activity. They are discussed in my books *Montauk Revisited: Adventures in Synchronicity* and *Pyramids of Montauk: Explorations in Consciousness*.

MIND CONTROL

In 1970, I built a studio out at Montauk. There, we were far more concerned about subliminals than audio function. Up to that time, everything was vacuum tube oriented. In the 1970's, the transistor reared its ugly head. Most of the studio at the air base was a solid state studio which meant the only way we had to do subliminals was through the extra head. However, the agenda at Montauk was much more bizarre and far-reaching than just adding in subliminals. There were a number of record producers in cahoots with this operation. They would sign up a group they felt might be popular and could sell a lot of records. Upon reporting to their local studio to record, the group was abducted and taken out to Montauk where a broadcast recording was made. After being programmed, they returned home thinking they had made the record at their local studio.

More or less around this same time period, I was also doing working for Viewlex, a division of a company called Electrosound. Interestingly, they had ties to E.M.I., the company who figures mysteriously in my other books (with regard to their seeming involvement in the Philadelphia Experiment and Montauk Project). I also made good money during this period by designing a record pressing plant for Electrosound. I remember that they erected a big building with the words "Gold Disk" on it. As I knew a lot of people at Electrosound, my partners and I were able to work out a sale of Buddah Records to them. They pumped more money into Buddah and kept it going.

I made a considerable sum from selling my shares in Buddah and utilized the money by experimenting in some rather avant garde projects that had to do with antigravity. Eventually I ended up working for one of the major defense contractors on Long Island. There was a lot that happened during the 1970's. I was not only working for the Montauk Project but holding down a 9-5 job and studying and experimenting with psychic phenomena. Still, my experience in sound engineering would end up landing me another gig in the entertainment business.

13

STAR WARS

In the mid 1970's, I was temporarily laid off from my job with the defense contracting firm. Before I could start to worry about my employment situation, I received a phone call from my old friend Mark Hamill. He said he was working for a movie producer who was making some sort of strange space epic and that they badly needed a sound man. He asked me what I was doing, and the next thing I knew, Mark handed the phone to George Lucas and I was being interviewed over the phone for a job. I heard George and Mark talking at the same time, and at the end of the conversation, George told me to get on a plane at MacArthur airport on Long Island. I got the job.

I flew on a corporate jet to a place in Death Valley called Furnace Wells. I soon drove out to Stove Pipe Creek. At least, that is the name I remember. It could have been something similar. Soon, I found myself involved in filming a movie. It was *Star Wars*. Mark was sleeping in a trailer and told me he had an extra bed. I stayed there and routinely found snakes or strange insects in the bed or trailer. It was as hot as hell itself, so I set up a big bowl of ice and water with a fan blowing over it because I could not take the weather. This was right next to the sound deck where I worked with all sorts of equipment and tape recorders. Twice, some of the crew thought it was great sport to dump the table with the entire bowl of water all over me and the tape recorders. Lucas hit the ceiling over that. The second time it occurred, he saw some of the stage hands who did it and four of them were fired that same day. Working on this film was quite an adventure.

When they actually filmed *Star Wars*, I literally saw two psychics or adepts that were concentrating on the camera as it was running. They were putting some sort of psychic overlay on the film. I recognized what they were doing because it was similar to what I had done with musical recordings. I assume that Lucas learned the technique on his own. Although it is not necessarily known to the public at large, it is not really a big secret that you can put images on film, audio tape, and phonograph records. I believe this is why the *Star Wars* movies achieved unprecedented popularity.

I had an opportunity to banter a lot with George. We spoke about sound and metaphysics. Mark and I both had some input on the concept of "The Force" that was used in the movie. This concept was introduced very late in the production. If you look carefully, you will see that not all of the sound of the dialog matches with what the people's mouths are saying on screen. There was a lot of dialog change done at the tail end, just before the movie was done. When you look at the credits of movies, you usually find the term "ADR operator." ADR stands for "After Dialog Recorder".

I found out that Lucas is extremely difficult to work for. He is very demanding and dictatorial. If something does not work, it is your fault, not his. I discovered that I was the fifth sound man he had hired, and although I eventually got the job done, George and I got into a shouting contest. I had enough of George Lucas. I packed up my personal gear and walked.

Upon returning home, my mother told me that my old company had called the day before. I ended up working again, this time in the microwave instrument division. A lot of this work fits in nicely with the Montauk Project. Eventually, I heard back from George Lucas. They wanted me back for the post production stage because I was the best sound man they had. I went back on a consultant basis for a limited amount of time so that I could keep my regular job. I stayed on in a limited capacity for the other *Star Wars* films, too. There is also another Lucas film in the can that no one has ever seen. It is called *Splinter of the Mind's Eye*.

I suffered yet another bizarre episode with George Lucas. I developed an idea about how to put digital sound on a magnetic sound stripe on film. This is known today as the "magnetic film track." I took this to Lucas and another executive. They both thought it was great, and Lucas funded me to develop the technology. I did so and it worked like a charm. It eventually became known as THX Sound. Later, we did *The Empire Strikes Back* in this system and played the first print at the Chinese Theatre in Los Angeles. It was called "Lucas Sound" at the time. I flew out west and set up the decoders in the projection room at the Chinese Theater. There were a load of people in the theater who were there to see the movie and hear the new sound. No sooner did I start up the system, but a damn radio station began blasting through the system. I think it was KTKA or something similar. It turned out they had a 50 kilowatt tower about a quarter of a mile from the theater. Lucas came in, heard the radio station and virtually kicked me out on the spot. I learned that anyone who works for Lucas gets fired at least once. He was a hothead, but he eventually hired me back again.

The episode with the radio station surprised me because the technology I had devised was supposed to be insensitive to stuff like that. There was nothing in the system that should be sensitive to a radio station. I told Lucas it was a total surprise and asked for some time to make a shield for the box.

After becoming the most heralded and successful producer in America by reason of his three *Star Wars* movies, George Lucas chose *Howard the Duck* for his next movie. That movie had very little commercial value, if any, but was loaded with subtle esoteric references, if you could stand watching it. It was never easy to figure out George Lucas.

The *Star Wars* movies themselves were based upon Lucas's own writings which were called the *Journal of the Wills* and was patterned after dreams he had all his life. The theory with regard to this is that maybe George is part of the group that came in from the Old Universe. His dreams could also be a result of mind control. There is a movie entitled *Dreamscape* which features a character named "Alexander," which is identical to Duncan Cameron's first name. It is about a government mind control program and is based upon an actual project called "Dream Sleep" where Duncan was used to access people through their dreams. One of his targets was Jimmy Carter.

I heard that George eventually bought a ranch out at Montauk. Originally, I had thought he had purchased the Montauk Manor or wanted to. I believe he may have been one of the original partners in the purchase of the Manor before it was turned into a cooperative/hotel. It is ironic that so many *Star Wars* people ended up at Montauk. Carrie Fisher married Paul Simon who has a house right next to Camp Hero. Mark Hamill ended up buying a house near Dick Cavett. The popular belief is that all these media people come to Montauk because the east end of Long Island is like "Hollywood East" or "Bel Air East." Others consider them to be "celebrity lemmings".

Mark wanted a house at Montauk, and I believe he bought it in the 1980's. It was designed by Stanford White, a famous architect at the turn of the century. Mark refurbished the house and it was gorgeous. I even had the keys to it for quite a while. One day, Mark and I were out at his house at Montauk, and I casually told him I was investigating the Montauk Project down on the old air base and asked him if he knew anything about it. He thought he was connected to it. He could not prove it either way, but he said that he always had an affinity for the air base.

I also recall recording the song "Break My Stride" with Mark during this general time period. He used the pseudonym of "Matthew Wilder," but it was him singing the music. There is also a touring performer by that name who sings the song for live audiences. This piece by Mark was different than most of his music written for Buddah Records which was very juvenile. Those hits were aimed at the kids. Although the words were often trite and corny, Mark's compositions were musically impeccable and very well performed. It appealed primarily to prepubescent teens. The fact that he could plug into that age group invites one to wonder if his music was connected to programming young people for the Montauk Project. I still do not know exactly what his connection was. For the most part, he was not part of the group that I was involved with at Montauk.

Mark also spent time with Duncan Cameron. They shared his beach house at Zuma Beach. This was long before I ever knew Duncan. They were doing pornographic films at the time, but Duncan ended up having some sort of weird surgery that left a scar on his midsection. It was supposedly an appendectomy, but that makes no sense whatsoever when you see the scar. It ended his movie career. I remember Mark saying that Duncan was the strangest guy he had ever known. He also said that he never ever wanted to see him again. Al Bielek remembers being "recruited" for the Montauk Project by Mark while he was in Hawaii in 1958. Al has made numerous attempts to talk to Mark but has never been successful. Mark is generally a very private person. He is not at all happy that he is mentioned in the Montauk books. I last ran into him at a mall on Long Island after *The Montauk Project* had first been published. There was no mention of him in that book, but he told me he was not allowed to talk to Peter Moon or Al Bielek and that he was doing a film for the government. I believe the film was "Philadelphia Experiment II." Of course, I have always mentioned that the Mark Hamill I knew may have been a different one than the current celebrity. False identities and duplicities are common in this field. Therefore, I can never say who is who. Everyone will have to make their own judgement.

I also believe that Mark made another recording that was sent back in time from the future. It is discussed in the following chapter.

CHAPTER FOURTEEN

14

SKY HIGH

In the disco era, in about 1975, a song was released under the title of "Sky High." The recording artists were really just a group of studio musicians listed as "Jigsaw." If you research the actual information concerning its production, as I did, you will find that this seemingly innocuous song has a very remarkable history. My personal discoveries led me to the conclusion that this song was recorded in the future and transmitted back through time and into the past.

My discovery of the true history of "Sky High" began in the early 1980's after I finished engineering school and returned to work at BJM, the made-up name I have given for my actual employer in the defense industry. Because of my vast knowledge of electronics and my involvement in the mind control projects, I was essentially king of the hill at that point and could pretty much do what I wanted. The rest of the company had rather strict dress codes, but nobody ever bothered me about how I looked which was not necessarily neat and tidy. So, no one said anything when I brought in a big vacuum-tubed stereo receiver and connected it to speakers so that it played

THE MUSIC OF TIME

music all around the plant. We primarily listened to CBS FM who often played the song "Sky High". All of a sudden, in 1983, it quit. There was no more Jigsaw; no more "Sky High". Quite a few of the employees liked the song, so we called up CBS and asked what happened. They told us the recording they had went to pieces and could no longer be played. They did not know where we, or themselves for that matter, could obtain a copy of the song, for purchase or otherwise. I put that information away in my head and eventually went to a record shop and ordered a copy of Jigsaw's "Sky High". It was a single 45. I took it home and played it at the correct speed, being sure to use a good needle that was placed correctly on the record. What I heard was the most horrendous cacophony of noise you ever heard. I did not know what that noise was about, so I returned it to the store. They played it and noticed that something was wrong with the record. Consequently, they took it back and ordered another one. Two weeks later, I went back and discovered the new record had the same problem. The clerk said he was sorry, but he was not going to be able to get "Sky High" for me. That was that.

    In around 1996, I was watching television when an ad came on for one of those *Time-Life* series of recordings. It was called "The Fabulous 70's" or something like that. The next thing I knew, I soon heard the song "Sky High" blaring out of the television speaker. I copied down the phone number and ordered the CD. Sure enough, I got the disk; and there it was, listed with all the other songs: "Sky High" by Jigsaw. After noticing that this CD was produced by Warner Brothers, I called up some contacts there from the old days and said that I wanted to find out the history of this particular song. I was finally referred to their tape archivist. This was a lady who kindly informed me that when they went through the master tapes for the different series, they noted an irregularity on the sheet that listed their master tapes. Next to the words "Jigsaw, Sky High" was the word "noise." This verified and restated the problem I had encountered years earlier. Finally, and for some unknown reason, the recording was replayed and the song could actually be heard. It was eventually put on a CD and made available for purchase.

What happened here? It took some time to figure out what had happened, but between my research and additional recovered memories, I was able to put together a tangible thesis.

The "noise" heard on the original master tape was indeed noise but was "white noise." In the book *The Montauk Project*, it was mentioned that white noise was the correlating function or "glue" which made everything stick together. White noise is basically a random group of impulses with different positions and different pulse widths which, when added to over a period of time, contains every frequency within the band width of 20 to 20,000 hertz. In other words, white noise represents practically every frequency that is out there. There are actually other frequencies outside of the 20 to 20,000 hertz range, and these are called "black noise," but we do not need to get overly concerned with the difference here. We are basically dealing with a panoply of frequencies.

So that you can better grasp the idea of white noise, take the mute off your FM radio and tune in between a couple of stations that come in clearly. You get a hiss. That is white noise and contains every frequency within the band width of 20 to 20,000 hertz, save for the fact that FM receivers are technically only 15 kilohertz wide so it

THE MUSIC OF TIME

really only picks up frequencies between 30 to 15,000 hertz. White noise basically covers the entire spectrum of frequencies. If you look at this hiss or white noise on a scope or spectrum analyzer, it looks like an infinite group of random pulses. It represents the cacophony of electrical transmissions that we know of as this universe. The reason you get a clear signal when you tune in a given radio station is that there is a device called a "limiter" which knocks out the noise in all stages of the receiver. This is called frequency discrimination. It is sort of a filtering process from the incoming carrier signal. Actually, the noise is being overridden by the carrier wave generated from the transmitter. The noise is still there but it is way down in amplitude and you do not hear it to any significant degree. Only the desired signal comes through and that is what you hear on your radio.

As white noise contains virtually every potential transmission and every quantum potential, it is a very open ended proposition. Within it are ordinary transmissions but also etheric and esoteric ones. It literally represents the energy stream of the universe. This is very common information to me, but most people are ignorant of the common facts of electromagnetic waves and too many professionals do not have a clue as to their esoteric significance.

The noise on the record "Sky High" was caused as a result of a closed down time loop that occurred in 1983. The Montauk Project was concerned about opening up a time loop between 1943 and 1983 as these two dates corresponded well to the Earth's forty-year biorhythm. This "forty-year biorhythm" can be compared to a meridian in the body through which life ebbs and flows in the stream of time. When this loop was opened up, it facilitated travelling to other points in time by the project operators. I eventually discovered that when the Montauk Project went down in 1983, the time loop between 1983 and 1943 closed. The "Sky High" recording was actually recorded in the future and was sent back into time. When the project closed down and the loop was broken, the song did not play anymore. All one heard was white noise which was actually the witness to the transmission of the song "Sky High."

The original studio master tape to "Sky High" was done at Montauk. One account indicates it was done around 1987 or 1988 where it was played and sent back in time to 1982. From 1982, it was transmitted through time back to 1972 when I was working at Bell Sound and recording something like disco. The song was actually very early disco. Another account, which I believe to be more accurate, has it being recorded in 1982.

When the hole in time closed, the recording disappeared. What was on the physical recording was basically white noise from the preamp to the tape deck because everything else was blocked out by the time transmission. The actual recording contained white noise that was a witness that called the recording in through time. In other words, if you took that 45 before 1983 and placed it on your turn table and played it, the white noise on the 45 became a witness to the original transmission of "Sky High." A portal in space and time was opened as the machine played back the recording, making a connection back to Montauk in 1982 where the signal was being transmitted into the audio system. The time transmission preempted the recording on the audio system.

As the record was made in "real time" in the 1980's, it could be heard thereafter. The theory is that if it was

THE MUSIC OF TIME

played between the time the loop was closed and prior to the original recording, it manifested only as white noise. When I have told this story in public, I have demonstrated the "etheric" component of the recording of "Sky High" by playing it on a tailored boom box I have fixed up. If you put your hand over the speaker, it will vibrate in a manner that you will not feel or experience with almost any other song. Two exceptions are the songs "Shannon" and "Beach Baby," but these are also believed to be time transmission songs.

"Sky High" was what we call a "time mark" recording. Duncan Cameron, the time traveller from "The Montauk Project," recalled having sign posts in time placed around what he was involved in doing. The "Sky High" recording, whenever that was played and the connection was made, was a sign post placed in time. Time travel at Montauk was done by moving from post to post to post to post, through an open ended vortex. This use of music was part of the time travel project.

Interestingly, I heard that a phonograph record that went out on one of the Voyager missions had Sky High on it. If aliens play it in the future, there is a time mark for their civilization, their galaxy, and so on. The time marker would be placed in their time which would become a witness to the Montauk Project.

CHAPTER FIFTEEN

15

THE MIND AMPLIFIER

The Montauk Project played a definite role in the majority of my activities in the recording business. Earlier in this book, I said that many groups were abducted and taken out to Montauk for their recordings. The mind control operations initially moved out to Montauk in 1969. In the early 1970's, I was handed the assignment of building a recording studio out at Montauk. I built a nice modern studio with all sorts of processing equipment that was of excellent quality. Since most readers are not technically oriented, I am not going to go into the details of it, but we had extensive capabilities. There were sixteen four-channel tape decks which were all synchronized together. There are a lot of advantages to having a lot of individual multichannel decks along with one big multi-channeled deck. With that type of setup, you can play all sorts of wild timing games between the tape decks.

One of the purposes of the studio I constructed was to pick up the sound and sight of what a person was seeing and hearing while sitting in the Montauk Chair. The Montauk Chair was basically a mind-reading machine. It was based upon sensor technology that ITT developed in the 1950's. It operated on the principle of picking up the electromagnetic functions of human beings and translating those in an understandable form. It consisted of a chair in which a person would sit. Coils, which served as sensors, were placed around the chair. There were also three receivers, six channels, and a Cray 1 computer which would display what was on a person's mind — digitally or on a screen. The chair room was about eight feet long and six feet wide. It was sort of a cubicle with a rounded ceiling. In the middle was a big lounge chair. Four coil structures were placed at each corner of the chair with other coils being placed along the wall. There were also four Altec 604 speakers in the room. We wanted to play music into those four channels and pick the music out of the computer that the person in the chair was hearing.

The purpose of the Montauk Chair was discussed in *The Montauk Project: Experiments in Time*. One of the primary reasons for its design was to enable a human being, such as Duncan Cameron, to think of an alternate reality and have it "picked up" by the sensor technology and in turn transmitted out the huge Montauk transmitter to wherever it was targeted. Originally, this design was to protect human beings such as those involved in *The Philadelphia Experiment*. The theory was that if the alternate reality was sufficiently transmitted to the sailors, their minds would be completely synchronized to the alternate reality and would not be affected by the invisibility experiments. Although this purports to be a benign form of mind control, it is obvious that sinister agendas made their own mark on this new technology. The Montauk Chair was in many ways a virtual reality transmitter.

Songs were recorded at Montauk and released to the public. The initial versions of such songs were never too

THE MIND AMPLIFIER

clear, but they were then processed through Duncan Cameron's mind and included the particular thought form he was generating. The final versions were always great in terms of their audio. It took a lot of work to get the decoding down so that it all worked properly. One of the more recognizable songs that ran through Duncan was "Everlasting Love" by Carl Carlton. It was used to put him in an orgone trance and set the mood for his work.

Although music generally sets moods, it is possible to incorporate different thought forms into the notes of the music. There is no question about it, and it has been done many times. In 1992, I did an experiment where I created a feedback through what is called a mind amplifier system. Basically, this device picks up the frequencies on the neural-net (short for the network of neurons that run throughout the body) by using audio frequencies. Once the frequencies generated by the person are picked up, they are fed back into an amplifier which amplifies the multiple frequencies of the person and sends it back through the output devices. This process continuously amplifies what the person is emitting and can also change as the person changes.

The history of my mind amplifier goes back to a device from the old ITT radio transmitting station in Brentwood, Long Island. It was owned by the Mackay company, or some name like that, and I was rummaging through one of the filing cabinets when I discovered a folder that said "Mind Amplifier" on it. When I saw that, I picked the folder right up and brought the information home. This gave me an idea of how to build one.

My first amplifier was huge. There were two chassis with a big power supply, and it took a lot to move them. There were two speakers and two input devices. The two speakers are set up so that they focus on the person at right angles. This can be easily visualized if you imagine a person in the center of a square room. The speakers would be placed at the corners facing the person and would be directed at their body. Opposite each speaker, in the two corners behind the person, are the input devices.

The inputs are pickup devices, like microphones, that pick up from the person's energetic field. Keep in mind that there is a human being sitting between two inputs and outputs. The outputs (speakers) generate auditory signals which mix with the human being and are then picked up by the inputs. Although audio equipment is used, the mind amplifier is really not a music system. However, its development was facilitated by a musical sound system that I developed more or less at the same time. This is the Biofiss that Peter Moon discussed in the introduction to this book and was the reason he came to meet me in the first place.

In some respects, the Biofiss and the mind amplifier are the same instrument except for the fact that they each use a different carrier system. The Biofiss uses music while the mind amp uses white noise for a carrier. The mind amp is not a music amplifier, and if you try to play music on it, you will get a very strange sound.

In the case of the Biofiss, a digitalized audio signal is coming out of a CD player. The digitalized "ones and zeros" are correlated into a wave form. That output is fed into a pair of vacuum tube amplifiers and in turn to a pair of speakers that are placed at right angles to each other. If you sit at the cross point of the speakers, as described above, you will hear a three-dimensional sound. This instrument is excellent for music therapy. I later on enhanced the Biofiss by adding the input network of the

THE MIND AMPLIFIER

mind amp. This was done in order to incorporate the white noise carrier into the system. By feeding the white noise carrier, via the input devices, into the tube amps of the sound reproduction system, I was able to emulate the mind amplifier. Of course, one also hears a pleasant musical sound which makes for a more pleasant experience. This device is not as "pure" as the regular mind amplifier, but it definitely does work in this regard.

Earlier, I stated that the inputs were pickup devices like a microphone. They were actually transducers from headphones. A transducer is defined in the dictionary as a device that transmits energy from one system to another, sometimes converting the energy into a different form. The input transducer in the mind amp was basically a microphone with a speaker in the box that generates white noise. This particular transducer is an eddy current device. An eddy refers to a whirlpool or circular motion. It you take a piece of steel or metal and subject it to a varying magnetic field, you will get a circular current flowing around it. The principle used in the transducer is not unlike that of a generator where the magnetic field is cut in order to generate a current flow. I used head phone transducers because they were basically a varying magnetic field that created a circular current within a metal disc. A circular current going around a disc sounds reminiscent of a flying saucer, but it just happens to be one of the best etheric energy transducers you will ever find. The disc is the metallic constituent in a microphone.

Flying saucers actually did play a role in how I used the transducers for the output speakers. When you are dealing with white noise, you are dealing with a very wide panorama of possibilities. Almost anything you can conceive is out there. Therefore, I wanted to filter out any negativity. I remembered seeing depictions of flying discs that were seen at Lourdes and at Fatima. On the bottom was an inscription that used the letters "I" and "H." I call it the "IH symbol," but it actually looked like this: ╫.

The IH symbol is actually an abbreviated version of "IHS" which appears on the back of priests' robes in the Catholic Church. "IHS" is an alteration of the Greek "IHΣ" with "Σ" signifying *sigma*, the Greek equivalent of our "s." The original Greek word was "IHΣOTΣ" which means Iesus, the Greek name for Jesus. The IH symbol means different things in Latin, most of which are incorrect. Although one can get more technical in the description of this concept, it basically refers to the consecrated host in Christianity and is a most sacred symbol.*

I used the IH symbol in the design of the mind amplifier because it is a sacred symbol of the powers of light and I figured that nothing dark would go through it. The IH design was integrated into the amplifier by laying out the transducers in the output speaker (or audio signal emanation box) in a pattern that looked liked an IH. There

---

* There is some interesting etymology with regard to IHS and the host. The dictionary indicates that the word *host* derives from Old French *hoste* for "host or guest" and derives from the Latin *hospes* but also notes that this word is akin to *hostis* which means "stranger or enemy." *Hostis* comes from the Indo-European *ghostis* which means "stranger or guest." All of this shows the words *host*, *ghost*, and *enemy* to be intertwined. Combining all of these concepts can be seen in the Christian teaching of "love thine enemy." This exact concept brings to mind the predicament of the Christ-Antichrist energy which has been a recurring theme in all of the Montauk books.

Additionally, the IH symbol is interchangeable with an early first century symbol which has been used in conjuction with the Pleiades: ✱. Still on this same theme, the consecrated host in the Catholic Church is reposited in a device called a "Monstrance." This word is akin to "demonstrance" as in "demonstrate" but is also a combination of the words "mons" and "trance." The word "mons" refers to the pubic or sexual region of the body as well as phonetically referring to Montauk or "mon" which has been explored fully in past Montauk books. It was a sexual trance state that was induced in so many of the Montauk psychics. (Notes by Peter Moon)

THE MIND AMPLIFIER

were three rows parallel to each other with another row placed horizontal to the others. In his psychic readings, Duncan Cameron had received information that sacred numbers have a sanitizing effect. Although this symbol was not a number in the regular sense, it was deemed to work on the same principle.

The white noise source (as heard on your radio when it is dialed between two stations) was fed into a preamp and multiplier before reaching the main amplifier. This process basically boosts the signal. Once the white noise was fed into the speakers, they would acoustically vibrate the speaker drivers. This would acoustically vibrate the metal diaphragm or disc in the headphone transducer and act as a microphone, thus picking up the psychic energy through the eddy current function (as described above). The white noise was the correlating source.

The is an overview of the mind amplifier. Technical people should realize that the description in the above paragraph is a tremendous oversimplification offered for the lay public.

The original mind amp was carted, with considerable difficulty due to its size, by Duncan Cameron and myself to Lake Forest, Illinois in the mid 1980's. There, we attended a psychotronic conference where I introduced the public to the Montauk Project for the first time. Although I was accosted by purported government agents who were adamant that I not talk about the Montauk Project, I went ahead anyway. We had a vicious shouting match which was witnessed by at least one attendee.

I gave a three part lecture at the conference. The first part was a short twenty minute lecture on the geometry of vacuum tubes. The second part discussed the Montauk Project, and the third part was a demonstration of the mind amp. Duncan demonstrated its use by first walking through the crowd so that the sensitives in the audience could sense what his aura was like. Then, we put him on the mind amp so that he sat in the cross section between the outputs and inputs as it was turned on. Afterwards, he walked through the audience again. The sensitives immediately reported that his aura had been amplified at least a thousand times. They also said that they could feel the amplification of his aura when I turned on the equipment.

The mind amplifier was a big hit. Almost everyone wanted to try it, and we had a line up outside of the room we were staying in just for people to come in and experience it. As there was not enough of it to go around, I promised I would bring one back to the next couple of conferences. As I did not want to transport that bulky monstrosity around, I constructed a more portable version. Instead of a 40 watt amplifier, I used a 4 watt amplifier. For the portable edition of the mind amp, I used a hybrid solid state vacuum tube system. The original mind amp was a string of vacuum tubes which take up a lot of space. This made the construction of a small device impossible until I realized that, in solid state technologies, etheric patterns are maintained in a device known as an "emitter-follower." An emitter-follower is a class of amplifier that has power gain but no voltage gain. When you are dealing with direct current, power = voltage times amps. The emitter-follower takes the existing current in the system, say a milliamp, and with the existing voltage, amplifies it to 100 milliamps. This gives a power gain of 10,000 with a voltage gain of less than one. In other words, it was perfect for a smaller unit.

Everything except the output stage of the amplifier in the small mind amp were emitter-followers. The multipliers

THE MIND AMPLIFIER

were emitter-followers. The noise source was composed of emitter-followers. For the output amplifier, I used 6688 vacuum tubes which I was already familiar with from Montauk. They must have had 10,000 of these tubes around the base, and they are good for etheric transmissions.

The larger mind amp was designed to amplify the thoughts of a particular person. The IH factor kept anything negative from entering the equation, but the smaller unit was not big enough to allow the IH design. As it had almost as much power, I had to be careful who used the device. Consequently, I ended up using it more as a radionics* broadcasting device. When I constructed the portable mind amp, I placed four transducers (the metallic discs from headphones) facing each other on the top of the box, and they acted like a radionics well. There was a small space, about 4 inches by 5 inches, into which one could place a radionics witness.**

At the same time as I was developing all this, I was experimenting with a Delta-T broadcaster.*** This is basically a Delta-T antenna with three fairly large audio amplifiers. As I already had a radionics input well with the smaller mind amp, I got to thinking. If I put something in the radionics input, it could be broadcast outward into the environment. I realized that if I took the x and y channel out of the mind amp and placed them into the x and y coil of the Delta-T, I would have something. However, there

---

* The term *radionics* refers to different procedures whereby a sensitive individual diagnoses and treats a patient through the use of an electronic device or template.
** A *witness* is an object from a person (hair, clothing, etc.) that is energetically attached to the person.
*** *Delta-T* refers to a change in time. "Delta" refers to "change" and "T" stands for time. A Delta-T antenna is basically an antenna shaped as an octahedron with three different coils. It is supposed to affect a change in time and is discussed further in *The Montauk Project: Experiments in Time.*

was still the z coil of the Delta-T, and I could not just let that flap in the wind. I then got the idea of connecting up the z coil with the white noise generator from the mind amp. Low and behold, I ended up with one of the most powerful broadcasters I have seen to date. I constructed a Delta-T that was small enough that I could fold up and take around with me and attach it to the mind amp.

As I carted this new portable device to different lectures, I did experiments which actually demonstrated etheric transmissions. At one psychotronics conference, I took a photograph of Swan Lake from the cover of a CD and placed it in the radionics well described above. This particular piece of music was written about a beautiful open lake in a beautiful backwoods setting. All of a sudden, the room cooled down 10°. People noticed the cooler temperature. Next, I took the CD of the music, stuck it in the equipment but did not play it out loud. Listing many different pieces of music on the blackboard, I went down the list and asked how many people heard each piece of music. When I got to "Swan Lake," which was one of the pieces on the list, about thirty hands went up in the audience. This simply means that those people heard that recording in their mind. It was being picked up off of a thought form imprinted on the CD as it went through all the processing from the original microphones, through all the digitalization and to its final encoding on the CD. By putting a photograph of "Swan Lake" in the input well, the music and the feeling of a beautiful clear lake were being transmitted throughout the room.

People can pick up the thought form of the music without actually playing the CD. It is well known that you can take a CD, a tape, or a phonograph record, put it up in the minds eye and literally pick the music the same way.

THE MIND AMPLIFIER

One is really picking up the extradimensional representation of the frequencies (or vibes). The mind amplifier uses a moving coil transduction to pick up and transduce the mind energies and amplify them. The mind amplifier feeds one's own thought forms back to oneself, amplified and clarified. It works by synchronizing your mind to the white noise. The transducers then pick up the signal that you are projecting into the system and feed it back to you through the same thing, but it is also amplified.

The Montauk Project concerned itself with manipulating the way different sections of the mind communicate with different realities in different dimensions. In this manner, one can control what the mind is thinking and what the mind is doing (in this reality). The idea is that the more you can get yourself into other dimensions, the more continuous you can be. Consequently, you would be less subject to anything in this three-dimensional reality.

Time travel at Montauk was basically an amplification of thought forms which were based upon the amplification of musical structures.

16

SHIFTING REALITIES

One person who most certainly seemed to be a part of the music and time experiments at Montauk was Jimmy Abbatiello. He came into my life through strange circumstances in his own life which I will explain a bit later. Jimmy is a fantastic drummer who played on many of the hit records I recorded out at Montauk. He even remembers some of them. When I first met Jimmy, I could see from his body language that he was involved with some project. He soon told me that he had a bizarre medical history. It turned out he was born with a defect in his urethra and has an incision in the area which indicates an implant. Doctors typically say they have seen nothing like it. He also has a hole in the back of his head which no one can explain. One doctor indicates it means he had brain surgery, but Jimmy is not aware of having such. Implants have also been found in his body which cannot be explained by normal means. After I learned of his various anomalies, I told Jimmy that the government would be extremely interested in him. Together, we figured out that he must be connected to Plum Island where all sorts of medical and biological experimentation is done off the north fork of

Long Island. Jimmy's connection to this was realized in part when he went to a medical doctor and found out that he had feline leukemia. This is a direct link to Plum Island because it is the origination point of that particularly rare disease which has no record of occurring in ordinary humans.

With modern reconstructive surgery and medical technology, it is conceivable that Jimmy could fix the defect he was born with. Unfortunately, there have been tremendous barriers to him fixing this situation. He has already received tremendous amounts of reconstructive surgery which claimed to fix him. Instead, it was used for an agenda of implantation. Jimmy is already quite a gifted psychic. If he were to receive proper and successful surgery, it would correct his sexual energetics which would make him all the more powerful. Consequently, tremendous hurdles have been put in the way of him earning a living and being able to afford the proper procedures. He feels that he holds the key to some information buried within him which will go very bad for his controllers if it gets out. Jimmy has also been told that he holds the psychic key to myself but does not know what it is.

I first met Jimmy as a result of a problem he was having with a man I will call Joe who had been administering some sort of New Age therapy to him. Joe used color, sound and had crystals all over his ceiling — all the trappings that can make for a good mind control clinic. Jimmy would lie on Joe's couch and receive etheric balancing treatments where it seemed as if time, space, and reality did not exist. After closing his eyes, Joe would wake him up and tell him one or two hours went by. Eventually, a psychic friend of Jimmy's met Joe and perceived that Joe was not all he seemed to be. The crystals and New Age therapy were actually a facade for mind control. Joe was living a dual existence and was serving some sort of reptilian agenda. The psychic said Joe had the soul of a lizard from Draco. Thereafter, Jimmy referred to him as "the Lizard."

After departing from the Lizard's therapy and company, Jimmy began to feel drained of all his energy. He said it was as if someone was beaming energy on him so as to kill him. As Jimmy never recovered from this "therapy," he figured his demise was at the hands of the Lizard who had a very powerful mind and was adept at radionics. The Lizard had some sort of radionics machine that was fixed up with antennas, synthetic crystals and gadgets which were supposed to make it super powerful. The Lizard's influence was suspicious because when Jimmy stopped the therapy and parted company with him, his mother became very sick with cancer. He also discovered a tumor which suddenly projected out of the side of his body from nowhere. He figured it must be the Lizard. When more of his friends became sick, he had other radionic people confirm that he and his associates were under psychic attack. Jimmy even went so far as to contact Charlie Whitehouse, a famous expert in psychotronics who did work for the U.S. Navy and built radionic machines for them. Charlie had Jimmy take a picture of the Lizard's house. Visiting the neighborhood as secretly as possible, Jimmy discovered that it was extremely difficult to photograph the house. Whenever he took a picture, shadows would come up. He said it was as if a force field was around the house. After viewing his exposure, Charlie Whitehouse indicated that in his entire career as a radionic practitioner, he had never seen so many evil entities or energies as were emanating from the Lizard's house. Something very weird was going on. Whitehouse confirmed it, another radionics practitioner confirmed it, and Jimmy's own testing also confirmed it. Everybody close to him was under attack.

When Jimmy told his problems to a friend, she indicated that he should contact me because I knew about the Montauk Project. When Jimmy heard the words "Montauk Project," he said he knew something was right. A bell rang even though he had never heard the term before. After hearing his story, I told him the "lizard energy" was used to abduct a soul for use in the projects. It is a common theme with Montauk people.

Jimmy might just be one of the first human experiments out of the modern Montauk Project. He believes he was a guinea pig who was part of a massive mind control experiment on the population. Someone was certainly interested in keeping him under control from a very early age. As a teenager, he attended Bethpage High School which is located right across from Grumman Aerospace, the premier defense contractor on Long Island at that time. One day, he went to his last class of the day. He was always the first one in that class as the room was nearby his previous class. As he sat in his chair, he suddenly saw hundreds of kids running down the hall to the classroom where he sat, almost alone.

Someone said, "Where's Abbatiello? Where is he? Point the kid out."

He had no idea what was going on. He eventually realized that someone said he had been masturbating in the bathroom. It was not true, but that made no difference. A mob consciousness had taken over. Witnesses swore on a stack of Bibles that he had done that and a lot more. He knew they were making it up. Soon, the entire school population, including the teachers, believed it. It was hard to convince anybody that he had not done this. Even one of the teachers laughed at him in a jeering fashion. He lost all of his friends and was isolated for his last three years of high school. It was a living hell as he had to fight for his life every day. He was hated and humiliated.

I have personally verified Jimmy's experience as I know other graduates from Bethpage who remember the incident. This is irregular behavior. Most school populations do not care that much about masturbation. Boys do it quite regularly at that age and are often caught in the school bathrooms. What happened at Bethpage is an atypical reaction. Jimmy had the following to say.

"I finally managed to get out of that damn school alive. I pretty much concluded they had to do something drastic to me because at that point I was becoming psychically aware. I always believed in that stuff. At that point, they needed to beat me down, and they beat me down so bad that it took me a good ten to fifteen years to get out of it psychologically. I am convinced that they needed something to keep me down sexually. Everything seems to be aimed at sexuality. They control you through your sexuality, your kundalini energy. At that point I was starting to develop psychic awareness of things. They thought they had to do something as I could be dangerous if I got out on my own. They had to create something so psychologically humiliating that it would put me in a state of shock and permanently traumatize me. It worked beautifully."

All things considered, there have been too many strange interventions in Jimmy's life for him to be a simple victim of circumstance. I also personally recognized him from Montauk. Another peculiar trait about Jimmy is that if I play some of the "Montauk music" that he helped record, his body cringes and goes crazy to the point where he cannot even hear the music. As these experiences occur, he begins to get back bits and pieces of his memories of doing various recordings at the Montauk sound studio. This is a very similar reaction to what Morgan, another Montauk boy, had when he listened to his own singing. Morgan also had memories of recording at Montauk, but he was a singer who was literally pulled out of the future to do some of his recordings. Sometimes, Morgan's recollections were actually from the future because he had not performed certain recordings in his current life. When Morgan and Jimmy were introduced to each other, they immediately recognized each other. A couple of days after meeting Jimmy, Morgan got more dumps of memories. The two of them together helped Morgan bridge a time gap in his own consciousness.

Both of these guys were at different times part of the Montauk house band. We had a studio in the second level of the underground. From what I have been told, they moved it to the fourth level. Myself and several others actually remember the bands. Actually, there were two house bands, and Jimmy played for both of them. I solidly remember him drumming in the band, and he also remembers drumming in these groups as well. As I said earlier, Jimmy is a good quality drummer and was even a bit of a local legend on the East Hampton club scene and is still remembered to this day. For years, Jimmy played every weekend for a house band in a club called the Krugerrand. Stars would come in routinely. He even played for Vice-president Quayle who took a picture of himself with Jimmy and autographed it. Some said he was the best drummer they had ever seen in the local clubs. He was on call and played with at least fourteen different bands. Although the fellow who ran Gurney's (at Montauk) remembered Jimmy playing there at least four times, Jimmy swears he played there only once. He remembers that in particular because he had to drive all the way out to the end of the island for only $75.00. The point here is that Jimmy played at Montauk without ever remembering what he did.

In addition to my own memories of Jimmy, I also recognized his drum style. Each drummer has a style just like each record producer has his own style. As a sound engineer, I had my own way of making a song reach out and grab you. No one else quite knew how to make it reach out in the way I did. Jimmy's style was also unique. It was an extremely accurate staccato style drumming. I could definitely tell the difference between him and anyone else. There are probably only about twenty real good drummers in the New York area, and Jimmy is certainly one of them. Unfortunately, there is not a tremendous amount of work for them. Nevertheless, Jimmy worked consistently until he met me. After that, he says that someone put the squeeze on him. Since discovering his role in black projects such as the Montauk Project, he has been consistently harassed and seems to find road blocks in every direction. Every time he had an opportunity for an audition, people were gung-ho to hire him. Then, all of a sudden, these people would mysteriously disappear. He said it was as if someone snapped their fingers and put him on a new planet. This happened with a man I knew named Art who was a vice-president and producer from Atlantic. He was going to produce Jimmy and then suddenly disappeared from his life.

Jimmy himself says, "What transpired here is that I was in this music project. They did not want anyone else to have me because then they couldn't be using me constantly. So, every time I got a break to do something that would involve me traveling on the road or getting recognition, they would get rid of the people I was involved with. It would happen every time. They knew I was as good as anybody out there, and they wanted to hire me, but it couldn't be done because of the Montauk people out there with their sticky little business."

This sort of operation also explains why Mark and Chuck Hamill were never on tour. They were being used. I believe Mark was also in the second house band out at Montauk.

Jimmy explained to me some very strange events in his life. One time, a show group wanted to take him to Las Vegas with them. They were impressed with his playing and hired him on the spot with a good salary. After being told to come back in a few days, he did so but discovered that the place he returned to was no longer there! After banging his head against the wall, he called up his agent who had sent him there. The agent said he did not know what Jimmy was talking about. He finally understood why his pursuers needed him. Jimmy explained the following.

"These people know that they are in trouble and they're going to get taken out. They've seen the future. They've sent me in the future to see where they can escape to and map out where to go. For some reason, I got an answer the other day. They need me to help them get out of this reality when the time comes. This is why they're not killing me or attempting to do any more than they are. They need me so badly for what they want to do that they can't touch me."

Jimmy is also very concerned that people want to study him as a lab rat. He is becoming more and more conscious of what has gone on with him which includes feelings of being used and manipulated. His controllers are losing a battle to control him. He is also becoming more and more psychic. This relates directly to his ability as a drummer because he can literally have some kind of effect on the consciousness of humanity. Drummers were not simply picked at random. They were picked for their ability. Jimmy was used because he was able to integrate his psi ability with his inherent talent and put out a psychic message that could be used for mind control purposes. His drumming style is a way of augmenting the mind control rhythm of the music.

I remember Jimmy going into a deep hypnotic trance as he played the drums. He was extremely precise and knew how to maintain a hypnotic beat with his drumming. That is why he was the drummer for two of the house bands. He was very good at it. Consequently, Jimmy was used for many hit records because his drumming put the listener into a hypnotic state. In musical programming, the rhythmist, which is usually referred to as the drummer, is the one that is most important because he is the one that is ready to put the listener into the hypnotic state ready to receive the program. In one respect, this is like tribal Indian or African drumming, however, many of these so-called "tribal people" do not really know how to do it properly. They just fake it. When people hear Jimmy play, they routinely say that they have never heard a sound like that.

It is for hypnotic drumming that he was chosen, and we have identified close to a hundred hits that he has played on. Many of these hit records came out of Buddah

Records and I remember them. Jimmy has told me that if you ask any of the stars who recorded the songs if they remembered Jimmy, they would flatly deny it. No one wants anybody to know what transpired in these recordings. Many of them were one hit wonders. The musicians never went on the road or appeared on television, but there are pictures on album covers with fictitious names. Jimmy said it would be a catastrophe if certain musicians admitted to his involvement. The connections roll back to the Mafia which includes their funding of such projects as well as other aspects of the music industry which they have their foot in. If big stars talk about their involvement in that, there will be big trouble for them, not only public relations wise, but their safety will be jeopardized.

As I write this, Jimmy is 43 years old but looks about 35. Physically, he should be past his prime as a drummer because youth enables one to maneuver a lot more quickly. His old hands are coming back which is quite strange. I believe he might be moving in time which could explain the renewed quickness and dexterity in his hands.

While some of this might sound delusional, it is not as simple as that. Actual people sent him to the auditions and then claimed that they did not know what he was talking about after the above occurrences. Even more bizarre was when he woke up to find that all of his body hair had been shaved off from the waste down. This was a change in physical reality that could not be explained. The most obvious explanation is that he was taken from this world to another reality. This is called reality manipulation or reality swapping. This might also be how some of the top bands were abducted and taken to Montauk. Whether UFOs played a role in this, I cannot say, but it is interesting to note that John Lennon had UFO sightings.

SHIFTING REALITIES

When one is transferred from one reality to another, it occurs during the same time. Time is continuous, but the reality is different. This explains how I could work at Montauk in a different reality than this one and still have a job in this reality. The key to the different reality is through time. In at least one respect, time does not really exist. Time is only expressed as the passage of one reality to another reality to another reality. If you think of time as a person walking through a forest, he is going through a series of instantaneous momentary realities not unlike what you see when a person moves under a strobe light. Time does not exist as such.

When you manipulate time, you are actually manipulating realities. Time is only a machination based upon what is happening to our reality at any given time. This means that when you talk about time travel, you are really talking of reality travel which is the same as reality shifting or reality swapping. I realized this when I went into the future as described later on in this book. Time is simply going from here to there in reality shifts. You can look at it as if our reality is a flat plane which for purposes of an example can be likened to a round pancake. As this pancake or circular plane moves from one consecutive incident to another, it can be visualized to create a "pipe" or "time pipe" of continuous incidents. As time is moving, that plane is moving through the time pipe and time is thereby defined by where the plane of reality is in the pipe as it moves from the past to the present to the future. In order to time travel, you have to jump from one plane to another plane within the time pipe. In the future, I actually build a device that is called a Jump Time Generator. It generates time jumps. One can conceivably move from any one reality to another.

THE MUSIC OF TIME

Although I have used the example of a pancake or plane and a pipe for purposes of making a more understandable presentation, it is really not that simple. The truth is that each instantaneous moment can be more accurately likened to a sphere. It is more like moving from one sphere to the next, but those spheres are in a bigger sphere which represents the time sea. As the sphere-like reality you are in moves through the bigger sphere, it can move in any direction you want. All time is one big sphere. And your particular time frame is just one sphere that is just drifting in a big sphere. Wherever it drifts, that is your ball of time.

Sometimes, a series of consecutive realities can be fed back on themselves in what is called a time loop where there is a continual repetition of events. There is such a loop between 1983 and 2003 where the events cannot vary. Duncan called this a dead zone. Technically, it is referred to as a millennium transition. 1983 represented the end of the millennium and 2003 is the beginning of the next one. The time in between is a no-man's land. We exist because the thought is still here, but we are not necessarily as physical as we were prior to 1983 or subsequent to 2003.

Of course, there were other bridges in time where one reality was connected to another. The next chapter includes a remarkable occurrence where I experienced such.

CHAPTER SEVENTEEN

17

SWAN LAKE

In an earlier chapter, I mentioned "Swan Lake," a very famous piece of music composed by Peter Ilyich Tchaikovsky. One of my first encounters with this piece of music came via my mother, Ginny Nichols. Her uncle worked in the theater in Manhattan and happened to be a close personal friend of Bela Lugosi, the actor who was famous for his portrayal of Dracula. Sometimes the two men would come to visit my mother, and she would call Lugosi "Uncle Bela." He once told her that when the movie *Dracula* was played, he insisted upon two selections from "Swan Lake" being played before and after it. Lugosi said that these selections would balance a person's energies after viewing the horror story *Dracula*. While this is an interesting anecdote from my mother's past, I have also seen evidence that those two pieces from "Swan Lake" can balance one's energies very well.

Originally, "Swan Lake" was a ballet and it existed well before Tchaikovsky was around. If you look at the choreography for the original ballet, you will see that the general theme of balanced energies is expressed. In "The Finale", there are two swans, male and female, on Swan

Lake. As a storm comes across the lake, a loud crash of thundering drums is heard as a lightening bolt hits the lake. Although the two swans are killed in tandem by the lightening strike, a vortex forms, and you see the souls go through the vortex and up to heaven. When Tchaikovsky originally saw this ballet performed, he was deeply moved. Consequently, he wrote the music, but as he did, he envisioned a vortex and it became encoded into his music. The theme for "The Scene" and "The Finale" are vortex music. I only came to realize this after years of research and discovery as regards Montauk and myself.

I have already discussed the fact that music is a thought form. Of course, many times authors will encode thought forms into the music without even being fully aware of it. As I did my psychic research, I began to notice a phenomena when certain people used the mind amp while "Swan Lake" was played. Sometimes the recording would seem to skip. There is no common explanation for this because it was a CD, not a turntable. Also, it only happened with certain people and repetitively. In other words, if you had them come in on Tuesday and it skipped, they could come in on Thursday and get the same result. Most people do not make it skip.

After a certain amount of time, I determined that the recording of "Swan Lake" that I was using was actually used to create the matrix for the reality we now exist in. If a person has experienced any time travel within that matrix, they will be able to affect the playing of the CD that had that signal on it. In short, this is a vehicle I use to see if one may have traveled in time.

According to this theory of mine, our entire reality was created via the Montauk Project. While I have recognized this as self-serving, I have repeatedly had to face the prospect that it is true. At best, I am completely correct. At worst, I am resonating with another truth which explains this reality more concisely. Better theories and stories are welcome, but I cannot deny what I have experienced and concluded for the time being.

At Montauk, we took the 1963 recording of "Swan Lake" by Arthur Fiedler and digitalized the sections known as "The Scene" and "The Finale." This was then used as the white noise carrier for the function that was generated through Duncan to create the reality we are now in. "Swan Lake" is the background matrix.

In *The Montauk Project: Experiments in Time*, I discussed that there are major biorhythms that run through the Earth's grid every twenty years. 1943 was chosen for the Philadelphia Experiment and 1983 was chosen for the Montauk Project. 1963 was chosen for an ITT project at Brentwood, Long Island. But, there is another happening in my own life that occurred back in 1963 which is right in rhythm with all of the strange synchronicities of Montauk.

Back in 1963, I was seventeen. This was a strange year because it was the same time when I had experiences with the Pleiadians (as told in my book *Encounter in the Pleiades: An Inside Look at UFOs*). After these encounters, my cerebral palsy became an insignificant factor in my life. Before that, I had been extremely awkward as a result of this disease. Additionally in 1963, I acquired a vast knowledge of electronics which I was able to literally grasp overnight. None of this made any sense from a "normal" perspective. In the summer of that year, I was involved in a high school summer session and was also part of the high school music group. The head teacher, Mr. Robert Milligan, had arranged for the high school band to go up to Boston Symphony Hall and be there for a

THE MUSIC OF TIME

recording session of Arthur Fiedler and the Boston Pops. I was not part of the band, but I was experienced and interested in recording so I talked to Mr. Milligan and got special permission to go on the trip. He knew I was capable in the area of recording.

When we arrived at Boston Symphony Hall, all of us kids got to sit in on a discussion between Fiedler, some of the orchestra members, and the RCA engineers who were doing the recording. Fiedler was grousing and complaining that when he took the recording tapes home and played them on his big sound system at home, he heard these awful rumbles. The engineers then played "Swan Lake" on the big system in Symphony Hall, and we could hear the rumbles, too. They were not all that bad, but Fiedler apparently had big speakers at home with big amplifiers, and the rumbling became accentuated. He liked a lot of bass. The engineers admitted that they literally did not know what to do about the rumbles.

At that point, I piped up and said, "Dr. Fiedler, I know what the rumble is, and we can fix it."

One of the RCA people said "You're just a kid. Shut up".

Dr. Fiedler was not so arrogant. He said, "Let the kid talk."

Immediately, I told him that what he was hearing with the rumbles were the vehicles and trucks going by Symphony Hall. I then pointed out that the microphones were on standard floor stands with no acoustical isolation. I told them that they had to go to the local department store and buy three stands that hold bird cages, each with a big loop. The microphones would be hung from the loops. Stands and stretch chords were soon procured, and I proceeded to hang the mikes from the stretch chords that

SWAN LAKE

were attached to the loops. They recorded a practice session, and sure enough, the rumbles were gone.

At that point, Fiedler took an almost instant love to me. He had me up at the conductor's podium as he conducted the music. I listened to "Swan Lake."

During a break, I said, "That's not the way it's supposed to be played, Dr. Fiedler".

He looked back a little surprised and said, "You think you could do it?"

"I don't know," I said.

He then told me to give it a try. I took the baton and began conducting with one hand. I went into a trancelike state and conducted the orchestra as they played the music from "Swan Lake." Amazingly, it sounded great.

He looked at me and said, "Where did you learn to conduct like that?"

"I don't know," I said. "It just came out. It just came out of me."

Apparently, Dr. Fiedler was quite a student of Tchaikovsky. He told me that I conducted very much like Tchaikovsky when his original productions were performed back at the turn of the century. It was the one-handed method. We spent the whole day on a shortened part of "Swan Lake." I conducted some of it, and he conducted some of it. What we actually conducted were "The Scene" and "The Finale," and these two pieces, with my conducting, were on the final RCA recording.

In the early 1980's, those running the Montauk Project decided to use "Swan Lake" as a musical frequency matrix to carry the time waves from the Montauk Project, and they selected the RCA recordings that I was involved in. This probably had something to do with me being used as a witness because I was there for the original

THE MUSIC OF TIME

recording. I surmise that they chose this particular recording with me present as I was also designated to operate a key part of the Montauk transmitter.

This music acted as a carrier for the thought form that was generated or actually created this reality which, let us say, runs from 3 million B.C. to 6,037 A.D. Each time you take "the end" of the future and feed it back to the beginning, it creates a path between the beginning and the end of time of millennia. Each time you create this feedback, you are creating what is commonly known as a superstring. There are different definitions for this term, but some of the renditions are hampered by the scientists' understanding of what is really going on. Some definitions are fine, but they are often designed to support different theories. They can also be too technical for the average reader. My definition of superstring is "a string of energy which goes through space and time." It defines our time.

Einstein theorized that if you move forward in a straight line, you will end up where you started from. This is a superstring. In reality, the first run through that creates a superstring would not have included an Einstein per se nor any of us as human beings. First, the original string would be something like a circular line (see "A" in the diagram on the opposite page). This is actually a time flow and that is the superstring.

What surrounds the inner circle and outer circle is what I call the "time sea" which represents time at rest. It is thought to be like a giant torus or doughnut, so I have represented it with two concentric circles. The time sea represents all quantum possibilities. That means all possible space and times are here. It includes all abstract information and ideas, including the universe of thought.

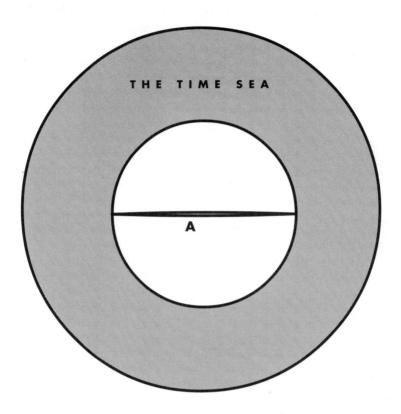

The astral plane would only be a small part of the time sea. There are no limits as to what it could include.

The original string created the first flow of time. When it makes its first connection, it hits the other side of the doughnut and could be considered to bounce back and begin spiraling around the original string so as to form a twister or spinor. This procedure adds texture and context until you have some form of matrix that might look like a grid matrix on the inside. From the outside, it would like a tube or pipe. We call this a "time manifold" or just a "manifold." It forms around the time flow and enables what we know as "human experience" to take place. The manifold contains a great deal of continuity and is a continuum all to itself.

It really all begins with a point of stress from the time sea. It is like reality forming as if to answer some idea of creation. There is no limit as to the number of manifolds that can be created or expressed from the time sea. All quantum possibilities could be expressed. This is what was meant at Montauk when we used the word "superstring." As I said earlier, there are many other descriptions by others which have validity as well. Each time you feed back, you create another reality and that fits through the superstrings. So, when a thought form was passed to Duncan Cameron in the chair, it was being carried by the Tchaikovsky Swan Lake matrix which went from about 3 million B.C. to 6,037 A.D. and created a superstring that generated another reality based upon the thought form that went into the original superstring. At this point, we do not know how many superstrings we have gone through en route from the Creator's original reality to our present day reality. But, "Swan Lake" and the thought form generated were a big part of it.

The "Swan Lake" recording that I participated in was released by RCA in 1963 and is roughly a half hour recording in its present day CD format. This is probably the best recording of Tchaikovsky's work that I have ever heard. You have to order it. It is entitled "Tchaikovsky's Swan Lake" by Arthur Fiedler and the Boston Pops, and it is on what BMG music calls their Victrola Series which was originally released as old recordings put on CDs. They were sold for $6 or $8 a piece ten years ago. I know they are still around because I know people who have gotten them recently.

Of course, I recognize that this entire matter is very strange. Here I was, a seventeen-year-old kid with no real musical experience or talent conducting an orchestra. My experience was basically technical. I had not gotten into rock music production at that point. What were the chances of me picking up a baton and conducting in a manner that was not only acceptable but was exceptional? Fiedler said that I used the traditional Russian conducting method that Tchaikovsky probably used. He was known to conduct single-handed.

Besides the above, I have had psychic readings and done many regressions which tell me that it looks to all the world like I personally am the reincarnation of Peter Ilyich Tchaikovsky. However, it is not that simple. I also have memories of being Preston B. Wilson, one of the Wilson Brothers who were involved with time travel and H.G. Wells. As the Wilsons and Tchaikovsky lived at the same time period, it should be recognized that I have encodings of their consciousness. Let us just say that Tchaikovsky was part of the Pleiadian consciousness that had come to Earth in the 1800's.

To the best of my memory, I believe that the recording of "Swan Lake" occurred on August 12th, 1963. This placed me right in the middle and at either ends of the superstring that went from August 12th, 1943 (the date of the Philadelphia Experiment) to August 12th, 1983 (the date of the climax of the Montauk Project). If the date is not exactly correct, it was very close to or exactly in coincidence with the biorhythm itself.

The story of "Swan Lake" is interesting, but it is not the only piece of music that is deeply involved with the mysteries of time.

THE MUSIC OF TIME

18

VICTORY AT SEA

As I grew up in East Islip on Long Island, my family was always very interested in and watched a television program which aired on NBC every Saturday and was called "Victory at Sea". It consisted of film footage of World War II Navy craft set to the music of composer Richard Rogers as performed by the NBC orchestra. As a young boy, I loved this music and had a phonograph record of it that I played to death. After a while, my folks had to buy me another record because I had worn the first one out. This one wore out, too, and I did not think my parents were quite ready to buy me a third record. Over time, I lost interest and no longer thought about "Victory at Sea."

A few years ago, I was watching television and saw a commercial indicating that the music for "Victory at Sea" had been re-released. I remembered loving that music as a kid and soon purchased it. As I listened to the music, I noticed something strange. I was able to return mentally to the time when I was listening to this as a kid with my phonograph and my little five watt amplifier and eight inch speaker. It was great nostalgia. I listened to it as I laid in bed and fell to sleep because that was exactly what I had done as I kid. For some reason, I dreamt that I was on the *U.S.S. Eldridge*, the ship that was the focal point of the Philadelphia Experiment. I dreamt that I was one of the sailors that were imbedded in the bulkhead when the ship returned to this dimension. Prior to this dream, I had experienced similar memories with various regressions. It was time to investigate this a bit further.

I started to play "Victory at Sea" for some of the Montauk Boys, just to see what they picked up when they were in a trance state. This fellow from the Midwest, who I will refer to as Bill, listened to the CD on my Biofiss system (as explained in Chapter 15) and went into a trance. "Victory at Sea" made quite an impression on him. When he came out of the trance, he reported that he and a bunch of other people were on a ship in the Atlantic Ocean and were diving for a crystalline object which he drew for me on a piece of paper. It was basically a ball with spikes sticking out of it and is called a "parallel-piped-vent crystal." He said they used this ancient crystal as a time travel device. They would park a ship over this crystal in the 1930's and then activate a group of short wave transmitters. In those days, what we now call high frequency was known as short wave. Then, in 1980, they would park the same ship over the same crystal with the same or a similar group of short wave transmitters. When the transmitters were tuned up to the same modulation and same frequency, the switches were flipped. This activated what is called the Einstein-Rosen Bridge. Basically, they were able to time travel by standing a boat over a crystal and activating it. This is how we actually shoved armies and technology from what we could call the present time back to the past.

This story from Bill explained a few things to me. It demonstrates how a receiver I built at work was transported back to the 1930's and was used as the design for the Super Pro (a receiver). I subsequently found this same receiver at a hamfest. It was being sold as surplus merchandise, but it contained all the notes I had left inside the IF (Intermediate Frequency) transformers so that I could identify it later. There are other indications as well that other equipment has been made in the future and sent back in time. I bought a little gyroscope from the John Roberts Estate. It was definitely a 1960's design, but the date inscribed on it was 1919. It was actually engraved in the body of the gyroscope.

All of the above suggests that we have had time travel back to the early 1900's. We believe crystals such as the one described previously were old crystals from the Atlantean civilization. Left beneath the oceans of the planet, the military discovered one close to South America located about 50 miles off of the northeastern coast of South America. It was parked under what they call the "Southern Cross." One of the pieces of "Victory at Sea" is entitled "Beneath the Southern Cross" which carried an encoded message that Bill, the Montauk Boy, picked up on. He was involved in some of the time travel. Consequently, I did a similar test for several other Montauk Boys. I told each of them that I had an interesting recording. They were instructed to go into a trance and just listen to it. After listening to "Victory at Sea," without any prompting, these guys picked up recollections of doing time travel with the same type of crystal. They also recalled being in some sort of embassy setting where they were attending an embassy ball. They described a room upstairs as being filled with modern computers. This occurred just prior to World War II. As quite a few Montauk Boys recalled very similar memories, I came to the conclusion that "Victory at Sea" contains encoded information of what we now call "The Southern Cross Project," an early time travel project.

I began to research "Victory at Sea" and sought out any traces of information I could find. It was very difficult because it was recorded back in the 1950's and there were not too many people around from those days. Finally, I happened to notice that the producer listed on the CD was Richard Mohr. That name was a little familiar because I had heard there was a Richard Mohr that used to work for RCA records on Long Island. I soon visited a retired RCA engineer who I had bought a lot of old recording equipment from in the past. Asking him if he knew of Richard Mohr, he told me that he was one of their producers from years ago. He was still alive and did not live too far away.

My next act was to visit Richard Mohr. He had a big house and a servant lady answered the door. I told her that I was interested in the history Mr. Mohr was involved with in the recording business and that I would like to see him. She was very polite and said that she would ask him. When she returned, she said that Mr. Mohr would be happy to meet me. She got me a soda, and I sat in his study for about fifteen minutes. Then, an old man came down the stairway and entered the room. He took one look at me and practically passed out. He barely made it to his chair.

"Mr. Mohr," I said. "What's wrong?"

"It's you!" he said.

"What's the matter, have I done something to you?"

"No, you haven't done anything to me," he replied.

Mr. Mohr recovered himself as best as he could and proceeded to tell me a very strange story. He said that when he produced the "Victory at Sea" recording, Richard Rogers came into the studio with a man who was the spitting image of me today. It seemed that this man acted as if he had written the music. Mr. Mohr said that the man interrupted the orchestra and began conducting. He was very emphatic about the way things should sound and was not always very nice about what he said. Richard Mohr swears it was me, complete with the gray hair, big belly and all that. Richard Rogers was apparently supplying his own famous name for someone who was an unknown in the 1950's. I realized that I must have written this music in the future and brought it back to the past, like a sign post, to help people recall the Southern Cross Project. Oddly, I know that music today like the back of my hand.

When Richard Mohr died, he willed me all sorts of paperwork about "Victory at Sea," but it is rather mundane and does not seem to indicate too much.

THE MUSIC OF TIME

19

SCIENCE FICTION

Some people have been quick to call my writing "science fiction." This does not make me unhappy because I am aware that the material is very controversial. Long ago, I learned that hard core science fiction fans and the establishment of that genre do not like such stories to be real. They want fantasy and fiction. If it is real, they reject it either because they are frightened or are serving some other agenda. Therefore, I have always told people that they can consider my writing to be science fiction if it makes them more comfortable.

There is no question that my work has been ripped off by the television industry, but it is always done rather cleverly so that I cannot easily wage a lawsuit. For example, there was once a show about mind control and time travel being done near a lighthouse. The word "Montauk" is never used though. There have been many other instances, but one is particularly significant in light of this current book.

As I write this in 1999, the Sci Fi Channel has been producing a new series of one hour long shows. One is called *Farscape* and another is called *Sliders*, an old show

THE MUSIC OF TIME

that has been picked up and produced again. There is a third one entitled *First Wave*. An additional one, *Poltergeist: The Legacy* is also being produced. As of October 1999, these four shows were shown every Friday night and rerun the next day. During the first weekend of October 1999, a very interesting and revealing episode was on *First Wave*.

This show starts out with a typical introduction that the "First Wave" is based upon the first, second and third waves of an alien invasion prophesied by one of the lost writings of Nostradamus. The general story line is about this guy who Nostradamus lists as a twice blessed man who is supposed to be the savior of mankind. He chases aliens around the country who call themselves some name like "the Consortium." The "blessed man" is usually chasing after something the aliens are doing. Some of the aliens are concerned with a biological agenda, others with a psychological factor, and others have a different slant altogether.

The first weekend in October 1999, *First Wave* featured an episode about the music business. There was a fictitious band named "Big Sur" or something like that and the producer of the band was an old time mix maven who just happened to be named "Preston". This particular Preston, along with one of the band members, was a member of the group of aliens. According to the story line, this Preston had built a secret device into the mix board that he used to record the band. The device was designed to trigger a hormone that comes up in puberty and will cause teenagers to go nuts and commit all sorts of violent acts. This adds up to a conspiracy that the aliens are going to put signals into our music that will manipulate civilization. I found this show very interesting because this

SCIENCE FICTION

parallels to quite an extent what I did in the music business. I was a master of mix downs and knew exactly what the public wanted to hear in the old days.

As the episode of *First Wave* continued, some of the band members wanted to fire Preston as the producer, but others resisted. They recognized that this Preston knew what the listening audience wanted to hear and knew how to distribute the music. The band members knew they needed him so he was kept on. At the same time, Preston was putting signals into their performances and recordings. The people who heard it went nuts.

The Preston in this show also spoke of wanting to put together a private label and set up a distribution system. Of course, you have already read about my involvement in Buddah Records. Although my friends and I never set up our own distribution, we tried very hard and eventually hired Neil Bogart.

This show obviously reflects my own work in the music business. The character had a different last name, but it is interesting that they used my first name in a scenario that is slightly distorted as to what I did in the past. All of this is very curious as the episode was written, produced, and broadcast well before the manuscript for this book was even completed. Did someone put this concept out so that when this book hits the market, the public would already have in the back of their minds that I was a bad man who represents the aliens? Perhaps it is a result of one of the production people I knew in the past who is trying to cash in on the awareness they feel the public might have of it. I really do not know, but someone is sending a message. They are saying that Preston Nichols is very famous indeed inside of the music business. Hollywood is notorious for the little innuendos of truth they insert into their mediums. In this case, they have lived up to their reputation with flying colors.

CHAPTER TWENTY

20

PYRAMID ROCK & THE LASER DISC

Sometime during the middle to late 1930's, ultrasonic scanning came into being. This gave the military a new toy which they used immediately. One of their first projects was to ultrasonically scan the entire country in order to get a beat on what might be underneath our environment. At Montauk, they picked up a disturbance. When they looked at the chart of the ultrasonic scanning, it looked like there was a huge rock pyramid underneath the village of Montauk. It was maybe a mile or two square at the base and two or three miles high. Concluding this was a pyramid, the military decided to pursue it and began a new project that would change Montauk Point forever.

In the early 1940's, I believe in 1941, Montauk Point was scraped flat. This project was apparently what obliterated the old Indian pyramids that were photographed and shown in *Pyramids of Montauk*. Although we are not absolutely certain, we believe these pyramids were at Montauk Point, not far from Camp Hero. The military built the Montauk underground at this point, mainly as a jumping off point in order to tunnel off to the rock pyramid

THE MUSIC OF TIME

underneath the village of Montauk. Four levels were built. Two were below ground and the other two above ground. The two above ground levels were covered with dirt and were made to look like rolling hills. Eventually, the entire topography of Montauk Point was changed. If you look at old maps of the area, you will find this definitely to be the case. There are even old pictures that show Montauk Point as a flat grazing land for cattle. Today, shrubbery abounds. They were "terra forming" well before this concept ever was commonly bandied about by science fiction fans. When they finished, there were four levels underneath the ground. They also rebuilt the gun emplacement bunkers during this period.

In the early 1950's, public attention was given to erosion of the shore near the Montauk lighthouse. In order to prevent the lighthouse from falling into the ocean, all sorts of rocks and sand were brought in and piled up to protect Montauk Point against the elements. This was very convenient because at the same time, they were building levels five and six of the underground. The tailings and debris from this project were used to shore up the land around the lighthouse.

It was not until the late 1960's that they finally started to dig tunnels down to the pyramid. Somewhere in the mid 1970's, they actually got to the pyramid and discovered some sort of doorway. Breaking their way in, they found different chambers. Inside one of these chambers was a sampling of ancient technology, presumably from Atlantis. There were huge crystal discs that measured about three feet in diameter. Players were also found that revealed the discs to be recordings. This technology was reverse engineered and eventually found its way into the world as the CD player which is in common use today.

CHAPTER TWENTY-ONE

21

ESPIONAGE & THEFT

I realize that some of you in the reading audience will be very curious about the mind amplifier or Biofiss sound system I described earlier in this book. Some of you will even be interested in purchasing them as well. In the initial printings of *The Montauk Project*, there used to be a blurb that anyone interested in psychotronic equipment could contact me at Space-Time Labs. This open line to the public was derailed due to some very unfortunate circumstances in 1995 that were reported on in *The Montauk Pulse*, a quarterly newsletter that is written by Peter Moon and has been regularly published since 1993.

On Friday, February 24, 1995 the facilities of Space-Time Labs were raided by six officials who claimed to be from the Food and Drug Administration. Two carried small handguns. They first found me and immediately told me that they wanted me to discontinue the manufacture and sales of biosondes. The biosonde is a radionics machine I devised that consists of a spiral copper coil within a wooden box. It can be plugged in to emit a certain frequency which is nil as far as normal electronics is concerned.

The theory behind the biosonde is that if you put a witness (meaning something that identifies a specific person, like a lock of hair or a photograph) in the coil along with something else, the second object will have an effect on the person connected to the witness. For example, if you wanted two people to fall in love, you would put both of their photos in the coil along with a heart or other love talisman. If you wanted someone to heal, you would put their hair or photo along with the proper herb or other healing remedy. You could also write a piece of paper with the words "good health" on it.

I never considered or purported the biosonde to be a healing device because it is too dependent on intangible forces to be of use in practicing medicine. In fact, I required customers who bought it to sign forms indicating that they realized it was not a healing device. I did note that people sometimes reported it effective for healing and also for ensuring good agricultural products. Even so, the FDA representatives claimed it was an unlicensed medical instrument. They entered my premises without a legal search warrant and claimed there was a new law that negated their need to have a search warrant if they suspected a violation of their laws. It is entirely possible that these people were not from the FDA but were using that as a cover story. They were harassing and intimidating in their behavior. As a result of this and further harassment, I closed down sales of any Space-Time Labs products. This decision has made my life much easier to live.

Although the above is bad news for those who might be interested in some of my psychotronic equipment, there is some hope for those who would like to experience some form of mind amplification. This involves a story which goes back to 1984.

ESPIONAGE & THEFT

At the inception of the International Tesla Society, which I founded with a couple of friends of mine, I did a lecture on quantum electromagnetism and performed a demonstration of the first bioelectric sound system. This was the forerunner of the mind amp and Biofiss but worked on the same principles. At that point, the sound system consisted of a large old studio tape recorder, a digital processor that I had built, a pair of rebuilt old Fischer audio amplifiers, and Altec speakers with some strange coils in them. The unit created a wonderful 3-D sound that was very well received by the attendees. No one said that I was all wet. In fact, most of the people who heard that sound system were amazed at the sound. The lecture went too well.

When it was time to return home, I packed up all of my equipment very carefully. There were nice wooden crates for the receivers and audio equipment. It was put on the plane in Denver. After a layover in Chicago, we flew to New York, and I brought it home. Upon unpacking the crates, the first thing I noted was four of the circuit boards in the sound system were no longer plugged in. The unit had four such boards that mounted vertically and plugged into sockets. The top had a piece of foam rubber to hold the circuit boards down on the main board, just like in a computer. The only way those boards could have been taken off is for someone to have taken the top of the box off. Then, when I unpacked the receiver, I spun the dial and it would not move. The reason the dial would not tune was that the idler that the knob drove was mechanically disconnected from the dial. Looking that over, I noticed screw shafts sticking up out of the intermediate frequency transformers. It was as if someone took a big hunk of wood and pounded them down. On the front panel, there were only two screws remaining out of sixteen that held it together. Someone had roughly disassembled this equipment and had done it in a very fast manner. Many other things were awry. The system was unusable and had to be repaired. Obviously, someone had ransacked my equipment, presumably during the layover in Chicago. An industrial spy most likely attended the conference and notified an influential superior who was able to cause a layover in Chicago that was longer than normal. This sort of thing happens in industry all the time. I did not get a clue about all this until about six month later.

The following winter, a friend and former coworker of mine applied for work at Alpine Electronics in Long Island City. As my friend was given a tour of the lab at Alpine, he noticed something in one corner that looked very familiar to him. There was a workbench with maybe a dozen chassis on it, and he saw what looked exactly like the amplifiers I had rebuilt and modified for my sound system that had been crudely disassembled the summer before. Asking what this was all about, the people at Alpine told him that they were trying to reverse engineer and copy a competitor's amplifier system. They said that they had made twelve of them, but they could not figure out how any of them worked. I could only conclude that Alpine probably photographed everything in Chicago. They were evidently trying to copy my amplifiers and duplicate the 3-D sound I had developed. As they were completely deficient in the understanding of esoterics, they were not going to be very successful.

Eventually, the parent company went from Long Island City to Japan and a one-bit D to A converter emerged from the Orient. This converts the digital signal in CD players to analog sound and is a replication of my original processor. The earlier CD players used an R2R ladder D to A converter. I improved the quality of sound by modifying auto-correlating routines originally worked out by Bob Carver, a man who designed audio equipment for an outfit called Phase Linear. Today, just about every CD player out on the market today utilizes a one-bit D to A converter.

Although the one-bit converter improves the quality of sound, it does not alone make a 3-D sound. I added vacuum tube amplifiers to get that effect on my sound system. This did not help the Japanese until tube chips were developed. A tube chip refers to a solid state transistor that emulates a vacuum tube. Tube chips can be identified by what is crudely termed a "vacuum tit" or "evacuation tit" coming out of one of the corners. They were created by the military and licensed to industry. The evacuation function removes air in order to create a vacuum. That is hooked to a vacuum pump and a space is sealed off so that the chip has an actual vacuum in it. The spacing is so small that you can get quantum effects with 60 or 70 volts that bigger tubes take 400 or 500 volts to get.

For those of you who are interested in having the best sound system available, you do not need to be directed to me. Today, amplifiers are virtually all "chip amps," meaning they utilize chips instead of the old vacuum tubes. Many of these chip amps, but not all, use tube chips to create an array of vacuum tubes in chip form. Ideally, you want an FET amplifier where the chip amp is composed completely of FET transistors. FET stands for "Field Effect Transistor" which is the first cousin or outgrowth of the surface barrier transistor. This was the strange transistor mentioned in *Montauk Revisited* that was produced by the E.T. Company on Long Island. If you have an FET amplifier, you connect it to a CD player (one bit D to A), being sure to eliminate that analog processing amplifier that comes with it. I usually connect the output jack of the CD player right to the output of the D to A and then to the amp. This creates a 3-D sound. Although it does not have an etheric image, it comes very close to approximating what I did with the Biofiss. As there are no audio inputs, it is not a biofeedback device.

It is not talked about in any of their literature, but I know that the expensive mini stereo by Denon has tubed chips in it. It is top of the line and currently sells for about $1,500. Some of the JVC equipment has tube chips, and I believe Aiwa uses them in just about all of their mini stereos.

For those of you who are obsessed about the mind amplifier and are wealthy enough to afford one, I suggest you save your resources. They are very expensive and problematic to put together. I once assembled one for a gentleman who was insistent that I build one for him. As he was willing to pay a considerable sum, I went ahead and procured all the necessary parts. I think it spooked him because I soon saw that it collected nothing but dust. It is not a toy.

CHAPTER TWENTY-TWO

22

THE RADIO BUSINESS

What you have just read more or less concludes the insights I discovered as a result of my work as a sound engineer. Of course, there are always more memories to unlock and new data to be discovered, particularly when we are dealing with the phenomena of time. For the rest of this book, we are going to focus on some of my experiences since *The Montauk Project* was written. I am aware that there is a big gap for the reading audience as far as what has happened to me since then. The reason this entire story has not been told up to now is that there have been a lot of problems with the circumstances and it was considered too dangerous to put into book form until recently. At least for the time being, things have changed.

This story begins in the early 1990's when the culmination of my experience in the music and electronics industries eventually led to me owning different radio stations. Although I had accumulated considerable sums of money in my various ventures over the years, none of these funds went into the radio industry. I ended up spending most of it on research and development of various technologies and projects. After speaking out on the Montauk Project and making a lot waves in the defense industry, I was laid off by my employer. Things were not going well for me financially when I met Peter Moon and we began writing the Montauk books. Soon after that, I had the good fortune to meet an old school mate of mine who would get me back in the radio business. This began a long and circuitous journey which was apparently designed to make time travel once again possible.

My experience in radio goes back to 1974 when I joined the Riker/Maxson Audio Visual Services Corporation as a studio and transmitter specialist. I was first hired as a "tech" and then a consulting engineer at Riker/Maxson. During this period, I became closely involved at one of the premier radio stations in New York City, Columbia's WCBS FM 101.1. This was when they began playing the "Golden Oldies." Their entire system was automated on what we called carts (of tape cartridges). If you remember the old eight track tapes, the tapes they used were similar except that they were four track tapes. There were huge numbers of these things in round cylindrical stacks. As the stack rotated, a mechanical arm took a particular tape and loaded it into the machine, played it, and put it back before rotating again to play a new tape. It was like a huge juke box. I basically put together this cart system at WCBS FM.

As FM stereo generators at that time were not very reliable, I set up a system for them which enabled the stereo encoder to be used once only for each song. We ran the cartridges at fifteen inches a second and set it up for half-track stereo. This refers to the format of the tape. One half of the tape is filled with one track. The other half of the tape is filled with the other track. I set this system up so we put L + R (Left channel + Right channel) on one track and L - R (Left channel minus Right channel) at 38 kilohertz on the other track. Therefore, all we had to do is take the two tracks, sum them and put them in the transmitter. This system did not become too popular throughout the industry although the entire Columbia Radio network picked it up from Riker/Maxson. We built a lot of them under contract to Columbia. Through Riker, I used to repair the CBS transmitter and also did a lot of work on their studio equipment. I was fairly well known at CBS FM from roughly about 1974 to about 1982.

It was during my work at CBS that I ran into an old classmate of mine, who I will refer to as Patty. I ran into her a number of times, and we recognized each other. Both of us said we had not changed much since our days in the eighth grade at St. Mary's. She had become a lawyer and had specialized in broadcast law. That explains her role at CBS. We became a little friendly, but I did not see her again when I returned full-time to the defense industry.

In 1992, I received a call from Patty. She had left CBS FM long since and had also lost her husband. She needed my help. Two of her attorney friends and her had purchased the license for 103.1 from Jack Ellsworth of WALK radio on Long Island. If I recall properly, they paid a million dollars for the license. In my opinion, they had overpaid, however, it was the last open channel on Long Island. Basically, they had run out of money buying the license and setting up the offices. She had no money to buy equipment either. Old FCC rules and regulations would have required them to post a security bond for $250,000 or $500,000 to ensure that they would be able to run the station once it was built. This was no longer the case. If you get an erection permit, you can build a station. Patty offered me a one-third interest in the station if I provided all of the equipment and agreed to set it up and run the station for the first year. As I was laid off, it sounded like a great deal to me. *The Montauk Project* was beginning to sell at the time, but these books have only represented a very modest income for me. I had enough money from savings to buy what equipment I did not already have or could build. So, for the first year, B103 (as 103.1 was known), WBZO was on the air. There was no one live at the mike, and everything was on total automation. The computer ran the two CD players, and the commercials and jingles were on the hard drive of the computer. I managed the station by tuning into the station on the radio at my house. Every so often, I went down to the studio, changed the program on the computer, and recorded new cartridge spots. I literally ran the station this way for two full years.

Suddenly, the station took off and became the sixth highest rated station on the island. As soon as we became successful, Patty and her two attorney girlfriends sold the station without consulting me. As they owned two-thirds of the shares, there was nothing I could do about it. They sold it to the Barnstable Broadcasting Corporation. I have always joked that this company has a brown thumb when it comes to New York radio. Everything they touch turns to manure. My shares, which at one point were considered to be worth about $750,000, went up to about five million over a two month period. The reason for this was that Barnstable had offered us twelve million dollars for the station. No one had ever paid that kind of money for a small FM radio station that had only been on the air for three or four years. It was unprecedented. The following bizarre elements and dealings in my own life have often caused me to wonder if this great deal was engineered by unseen powers in order to assist me in accomplishing certain things. This possible angle will become more apparent as my story continues.

I was already familiar with the Barnstable company because I had already done business with them. When they purchased IBC, the old Island Broadcasting Company, there were some stations they acquired that were doing poorly. As they did not want them, I purchased them and built them up with the dividends I received from B103. When B103 was sold, I lost my dividends and could no longer afford to maintain the stations. I was able to swap them back to Barnstable for some stock in the company. I could not use the money acquired from the sale of B103 for tax reasons that I will explain later.

I stayed on at B103 as Broadcast Executive Consultant, but I only dealt with technology. This went on for about two years. It was not too long after Barnstable had purchased B103 that they decided they wanted to sell it. The supposed reason for this was that they wanted to purchase 103.5 in Manhattan. There were regulations at the time with regard to how many radio stations could by owned by one company in the New York market. In order to buy 103.5, they needed to shed a few stations. By that time, B103 had gone way down in the ratings to number twelve or thirteen. As I still had stock in the company at this point, the vice-president of Barnstable, Mikee Conet, approached me and asked if I wanted to buy the B103 operation. We negotiated and agreed upon a deal where I paid about six million for two-thirds of the stock.

Of course, you might wonder why I would want to buy a station for so much money when I had just received a large cash payout. There was actually a very good reason. It is called taxation. If I had "cashed in" my profits, I would have walked away with very little after capital gains and windfall profit taxes. Believe it or not, there would have been only about $800,000 left over. One legal solution to employ in such a matter is something called a "capital corporation" which is a sort of tax shelter. In other words, the money can be placed in the corporation's account which can then be used to buy other capital property. It could be more deftly explained by an accountant, but the idea is to legally avoid capital gains taxes until the time that the money is finally cashed in. Besides not paying extremely high taxes, I could also declare dividends at the end of each quarter and receive an income. Although there were taxes on the income, it was next to nothing compared to the huge capital gains and windfall taxes that would have been levied otherwise. In this method of sheltering taxes, there is a statute of limitations determined by the IRS for each case. It is usually about three to seven years. Once that is exceeded, you can take out whatever money you want and only have to pay regular income taxes. I have oversimplified the entire matter. Each case is different and you should consult an accountant if you are interested in pursuing any of these avenues yourself. Basically, these are rules that wealthy people use to avoid paying huge taxes.

  As Barnstable still owns one-third of the station, it is still listed as a Barnstable affiliate. I control the executive decision making process. This is good because, as I said, they have a brown thumb. When I came back, I discovered they had only a thirty song play list. Not only that, the songs repeated themselves daily. In other words, if you tuned at 10:00 a.m. one morning and heard a song, you would hear it the next day at the same time. This was corny and hurt the station. The staff did not want to add to the play list because it would require additional copyright reports and that sort of thing. I told them to put a "shuffle" on their computer so that it would at least move the songs about randomly. Eventually, the number of songs were increased and the station recovered.

There was a lot of wheeling and dealing that went on during this period, and I have certainly not recounted every last detail. One of the vehicles my accountant set up for me was a real estate trust. I was advised to diversify some of my assets in real estate. Accordingly, I went to a big real estate broker and told them I wanted to buy a strip mall. I had about two million dollars to spend for this purchase. They told me I could pick up about six stores for that price. About three weeks later, the broker called me and said he had a fantastic deal for me. They were just handed a mall to sell. It had about twenty stores and was located near Port Jefferson. There were three owners and one of them had just died. In order to settle the estate, they had to sell the property very fast. If I could come up with a million and half, which was well below the book value, I could buy the mall. I checked it out and found it to be a very good deal. The title search was done, and I was soon the owner of a shopping center.

Six months later, this gentleman with a Jewish name approached me and informed me that I owned another building on the outskirts of the mall parking lot. It was occupied by the phone company who had built the structure to their own specifications and leased it for a period of thirty years. Actually, as it turned out, I did not own the building. I owned the property that the building was on. This issue was coming up because the thirty year lease had expired. The phone company was supposed to be moving. The man himself actually owned the building and wanted to sell it to me. I was not interested. As this man was motivated to sell, he offered me the building plus four other industrial buildings behind it. It was a good deal for about one million dollars, and I ended up owning the whole corner. The next thing I knew, I am approached by FG Industries. They wanted to buy the whole corner and offered me eight million dollars. It was too much to refuse. I ended up selling the entire shopping center as well as the corner property they originally wanted.

After reading this, most of you will think that I am an exceptional business person, but I do not consider this to be the case. Most of my activities were precipitated by good advice from accountants, lawyers, and just plain good fortune. The other side of the coin is that most of what I acquired was only paper wealth. It did not fatten my personal bank account. Earlier, I alluded to the idea that perhaps some unseen forces were working in the background to assist me. You see, if you give a person like me vast sums of money, I can tinker with all sorts of equipment and produce all kinds of interesting effects. Of course, this includes time travel research. If there were indeed forces that were trying to help me, it soon became apparent that there were other forces which were not so friendly. These forces showed their ugly face in 1996 when my friend and associate, John Ford, was unexpectedly arrested and jailed.

CHAPTER TWENTY-THREE

23

JOHN FORD ARRESTED

Many people who are serious investigators of UFOs have heard the name of John Ford. For those of you who are not familiar with him, John Ford was the president of the Long Island UFO Network, a nonprofit enterprise that he himself founded along with Richard Stout. John was a very high profile investigator of UFOs on Long Island. He made a lot of waves and was extremely thorough in his investigations, sometimes to the point of boredom. He often called on me to help with his investigations, particularly with regard to surveying the electromagnetic fields where UFOs had reportedly crashed. We had worked together for many years.

On the 13th of June in 1996, I was scheduled to go to John Ford's house. Before I left for his house that day, I received a phone call from an unidentified lady in upstate New York who warned me not to go. She indicated there would be trouble for me if I did. I took the hint and stayed at home. On that very evening, John Ford and Joseph Mazzuchelli were arrested and jailed by the Suffolk County police with a list of different charges. Another man, Edward Zabo, was later arrested as well. The most bizarre charge was that they had conspired to poison and kill John Powell, the Republican party chief in Suffolk County, by placing radium in his toothpaste. Although this sounds comical and is virtually impossible to accomplish, the arrest made headlines and was covered as the lead story on most of New York's major television stations. It was big news. Other charges included possession of an illegal substance (radium) and illegal firearms. The District Attorney arranged to have media people on location as video tapes were shown of the inside of John's house and included a panning of his sizable gun collection. This was an apparent attempt to make him look like a "militia wacko." To almost everyone's surprise, John was never a member of the militia, and all of the firearms he owned were acquired legally and registered. He is a collector of guns. The prosecution and media had to back off on this charge right away, but they never corrected their mistake. The media only reported the prosecution's version.

    These were very sad and distressing times for myself and anyone who knew John Ford. He soon phoned me from jail as I was virtually his only contact on Long Island who could help him. His mother had died in the recent past. He also had a brother and sister who lived out of state, but they were not particularly sympathetic towards his views about UFOs. This meant that I was the one elected to go to his house and see that his pets were taken care of and that no vandalism or other problems occurred.

    Ford's bail bond was a whopping $500,000 which the prosecutors knew he could not possibly meet. Typically, when a person is arrested on suspicion of murder, their bond is set at about $100,000. Ford was only suspected of conspiring to commit murder by placing radium in a toothpaste tube, a laughable prospect at best.

JOHN FORD ARRESTED

No one had been killed, and certainly no one believed that such a scheme would work, even if it were seriously attempted. I knew John well enough to know that he was not interested in killing anyone.

All of the above prompted many questions. It was all too weird. The motivations behind the arrest of John Ford seemed entirely political. After all, his mother had been a pivotal character in politics for years. John Ford himself was very much involved in the Conservative Party which is very closely tied to Republican politics. His main rival was John Powell, the party chief who was the alleged target of an "assassination by toothpaste." It was very funny except for one important point. John Ford was incarcerated with no possible hope of release.

As I went about taking care of John Ford's personal effects, Peter Moon began focusing on the facts of the situation with particular regard to the legal justification for the arrest. Deputy District Attorney, Martin Thompson, claimed that an informant in the weapons case alerted authorities of the murder plot on Wednesday, June 12th. Later that day, authorities taped the conversations during which they claimed to have overheard Ford and Joseph Mazzuchelli discuss the plot. The two were soon arrested. This raised a curious question. How would the informant have knowledge of such a plot? Were Ford and his buddies advertising for hit men? Thompson said that Ford's conversations were recorded. If this were true, this would have been accomplished by bugging or phone tapping. In either case, a warrant would have to be authorized. Electronic bugging would entail going onto Ford's property.

After considering the above information, Peter called me and asked if there was a search warrant. As the arresting officers had left a copy at Ford's house, I had already made my own copy. While answering Peter's question, I noticed that the search warrant was dated after the arrest had taken place. Eventually, the D.A.'s office reported that the date on the warrant was incorrect. When John Ford's lawyer, John Rouse, asked for a copy of the warrant, it was a different warrant than the one I had obtained from Ford's premises. Rouse filed a motion charging the prosecution with filing an insincere document, but the judge dismissed it. This was just the tip of the iceberg as far as funny circumstances surrounding the arrest of John Ford were concerned. Two different reporters investigated the matter and came up with astonishing revelations, but no one would publish their findings. They were too politically volatile.

What was disturbing to me was that someone wanted John Ford taken out of circulation. Whoever that was apparently wanted me taken out, too. I was scheduled to be at Ford's house on the evening of his arrest and was probably slated for jail as well, but I had a lot more luck going for me. I received a phone call before the meeting telling me not to go. A lady told me there would be trouble for me if I did. I heeded the warning and have never regretted it.

As the situation with John Ford's arrest unfolded, Peter Moon continued to tackle the irregularities in the case and published his findings in *The Montauk Pulse*, a quarterly newsletter which reports on developments and circumstances with regard to the Montauk Project. I was not so sure and thought the information might be too dangerous to put into print. There had already been one attempt on my life, and I had directly worked for Ford's Long Island UFO Network as a scientific consultant.

JOHN FORD ARRESTED

I consulted one of my friends who I refer to as "the Colonel." He served in special forces in the Air Force and is also a nuclear physicist. I met him in my consulting business many years ago when he happened to mention the Montauk base and said that he had worked there. He told me about going down an elevator to the underground where he would service their vacuum tube equipment as an independent contractor. He even told me the exact location where he was taken to access the elevator. It was a small blue wooden building in what is now a grassy field south of the tennis courts at Camp Hero. I knew about the building because I have pictures of it from my initial investigations of the base back in the late 1980's. It was demolished years ago, and there is now no longer any trace of the building. The Colonel took some interest in my stories, but we also had a professional relationship. We complement each others' knowledge quite well. He is an expert in nuclear physics, and I am an expert in electromagnetism. While we both know a lot about each others' fields, there is always more to learn for both of us. Although he has acted as a friend and has definitely protected me over the years, I still have not completely figured him out. He did tell me that he is still connected to Air Force Intelligence.

With regard to John Ford, the Colonel informed me that there was a lot of trouble brewing in Suffolk County politics. Stories circulated indicated that Suffolk County had gotten far too big for its britches. They had become a rogue element all to themselves and even had plans to secede from New York State and even the United States of America. While this might seem farfetched to some, there was a major publicized effort for a new county to be formed on the east of end of Long Island that would include East Hampton and Montauk. It was to be called Peconic County, but thus far, that movement has been defeated. John Powell, the man who was allegedly targeted by John Ford in the toothpaste plot, was known to be the most powerful man in Suffolk County. His nickname was "Bugsy," and as the political boss of the Republican Party, he oversaw who would represent the party in elections, including judges. Needless to say, the situation between Ford and Powell was intense and there was a lot of power behind the latter.

Whether or not the thesis about Suffolk County wanting to secede from the United States of America was true, there were some pretty strange goings on. Additional revelations came to light when Peter Moon was told by an informant within the legal system that radioactive waste from Camp Hero was being dumped in the East Hampton Town dump. Peter was told not to tell anyone as "someone could get killed." John Ford not only knew a lot about county politics, he also knew a lot about illegal dumping of toxic waste. His home was very close to the Brookhaven Town landfill, and there was a movement to declare his property, along with that of his neighbors, emminent domain so that it would be sold and used to expand the town dump. He and some of his neighbors had already begun a grass roots movement to counter this effort. Without any reference to his UFO investigations, his knowledge of these things alone was enough to make him a target for his political opponents.

Ford's primary political opponent was the alleged target of the "assassination attempt," John Powell, one of the most powerful Republicans in New York and certainly the political leader of Suffolk County. Powell was described in the newspaper for even being able to make the

New York Governor "jump." He bragged that when he phoned Pataki, the Governor had to take his calls. The reason for this at least has something to do with the fact that without Powell's political influence and voter support, Pataki would never have won the election for Governor. If there is a stronger connection behind the scenes, I do not know. But, Pataki was reported in *Newsday* to have been one of the first to offer his sympathies and concern when Powell was supposedly targeted for assassination by John Ford.

In the midst of all this political stuff, I received a phone call from the Colonel who told me to watch a rerun of a 1994 episode of *Northern Exposure*, a television show that was scheduled to appear on a cable channel. The entire episode was surreal in that it was too hauntingly familiar to the John Ford scenario to be an accident. The show featured a conspiratorial rabblerouser who wore army fatigues and possessed a personality that was something of a combination of John Ford and myself with some extra zaniness thrown in as well. The rabblerouser was blowing the whistle on a fireworks dealer from Maspeth, New York who was dealing arms in connection with the Iran-Contra scandal. The thesis was that a fireworks manufacturer could easily smuggle or ship fire arms under the umbrella of regular commerce. In other words, where do fireworks end and firearms begin? In the show, the bad guys were trying to put the rabblerouser in a sanitarium on the grounds of being mentally incompetent. Boy, did this sound familiar. John Ford was eventually declared mentally incompetent and never received a trial with regard to the accusations made against him.

Although the television show revealed many coincidences to the John Ford case, the reference to a fireworks dealer was a new twist. It just so happens that one of the biggest and most prestigious fireworks dealers in the world is located on Long Island not too far from the city of Maspeth, New York. John Ford's nemesis, John Powell, was known to be allied to a Long Island fireworks manufacturer.

Whatever the actual truth and circumstances were, here was a television show from 1994 making an oblique reference that covert arms dealing was taking place on Long Island. The show was certainly prophetic with regard to an attempt to have John Ford declared mentally incompetent and put in a sanitarium. It was years ahead of its time with regard to that. How did the television writer "pick up" on this? John Ford had not even been arrested at the time the show was originally produced. Was this a simple coincidence or was somebody using the television industry to deliver a message? And, here I was being tipped off about the show through a man in Air Force intelligence. As this story unfolds, you will see that it is entirely possible that the message from this show actually came from the future and was somehow, subconsciously or otherwise, leaked through the television industry.

In the meantime, no one needed to watch a television show to understand that there were some major problems on Long Island.

CHAPTER TWENTY-FOUR

24

THE AIR FORCE

Even though I once suffered a severe accident under very suspicious circumstances (see *Encounter in the Pleiades* for a description), I did not realize that at the time of his arrest, John Ford's problem was actually my problem. I now realize that I was also a major target of the arrest.

I believe it may have all begun back in 1992 during the investigation of the South Haven Park crash. This was a UFO crash that occurred in a public park which is practically in the backyard of Brookhaven Labs. John received information which led him to believe that a ship came in and dropped some pods before eventually crashing at the lab. Although we did not have access to Brookhaven Labs, we were able to look all over South Haven Park and the property which is right behind police headquarters in Yaphank. We were looking right under the nose of town officials who owned property right next to this location. Consequently, we were seen by a lot of Brookhaven town people as we investigated on county property. Although we were just nosing around for UFO debris, we certainly would have alerted anyone who had anything to hide. In retrospect, this made us all potential targets for retaliation. UFO investigation did not necessarily have anything to do with it. However, it should be mentioned that the bridal trails at South Haven Park were inaccessible the day after the crash as the Army occupied the territory, presumably doing a cleanup of UFO debris.

At the same time, John Ford and his neighbors had formed a political committee to stop the expansion of the town garbage dump. The dump has a buffer zone around it which separates it from the community. The town wanted to take this buffer zone and designate it as "Cell Number 3" and use it for dumping. In turn, John Ford's property, as well as that of his neighbors, would be designated the new buffer zone. During this time, one of the local ladies who was a part of this committee took a job working as a receptionist at the town dump. She kept a private diary of who came and went and noted what was being carried in. That is probably what the police were looking for when they searched John's house at the time of his arrest. They literally tore the place apart. As this story unfolds, this aspect with regard to the town dump will become much clearer.

Anyone watching us at South Haven park that day might have also seen my two-tone blue van with antennas on the roof and scientific equipment in the back. It was parked at John Ford's off and on that day. Most people would look at my contraptions and not have the slightest idea what it actually is. That would have spooked any observers who surely would have reported it. As we were also near the dump, they probably figured I had been sent in with environmental equipment to sample the air and get data for John Ford and his ad hoc committee which they surely knew about.

It was after this time period that someone began to repeatedly loosen the lug nuts on my vehicles and so try to

THE AIR FORCE

cause an accident. I had a lot of run-ins with different officials including the police. I did not feel safe and sought out whatever protection I could find. Finally, I consulted my friend who I call the Colonel. He and the group he represented wanted to keep my rear end out of the fire. In order to protect me and to keep me from being arrested like John Ford, they provided protection which allegedly came through the Air Force. I was given an 800 number that I could call if things got too tight. I used this more than a few times, and it even saved me from being arrested on one occasion. As I was being taken into custody, military policemen miraculously appeared and superceded the local police force that was involved. I was told that I was receiving protection from the Air Force because I was one of only four people on the planet who really understood time. This makes me an indispensable resource as far as they are concerned.

THE MUSIC OF TIME

CHAPTER TWENTY-FIVE

25

DECLARED INCOMPETENT

John Ford was not going to sit in jail forever. After being in jail for over a year, the *Northern Exposure* TV show was to prove as prophetic as ever. After a psychiatric examination, he was declared incompetent to defend himself. His lawyer was suggesting an insanity plea. John was told this was a stall tactic, and we learned that he was not in agreement with actually pleading "mental incompetence." According to his own statements, John Ford was tricked. After the examination, John was legally declared mentally incompetent and had no real power to even change his attorney.

Whether or not John Ford's claims about UFOs and the like are true, we do know that he was a diligent researcher who left no stones unturned. His lectures were sometimes very dry, but they were thorough. The files that he had worked so hard to collect for so many years were confiscated and no one knows what has happened to them. The doctors did not mention this in their reports! Fortunately, some of his most precious information was hidden between the walls and was later recovered by a friend. Nobody fully understands the entirety of what John Ford knew. One of the reasons for this is that he kept too many secrets. As is the case with many intelligence operatives, he was a hoarder of information.

Regardless of the UFO claims, we do know that John was receiving drugs in prison. Part of this had to do with a back condition, but I noticed pronounced mood changes during my frequent visits. I was concerned that they were drugging him in order to make him more docile and agreeable to an insanity plea. Such a plea would diffuse anything he had to say because people could consider him to be insane.

To make matters worse, John was to be shipped off to the Mid-Hudson Sanitarium, a facility that is for the criminally insane. This means axe murderers and the like. He had already lost his pets, his house, and his research. Now, he was being sent to a place from which he has, as of this date, never returned. Even though John was being sent off to the sanitarium, he felt somewhat relieved. His "incompetent" status meant the D.A. could not prosecute him, at least for the time being. At the hearing prior to him being sent away, the D.A. reserved the right to prosecute him at a later date. Keep in mind that John Ford was never convicted of any crime. He was accused, incarcerated, and funneled into a sanitarium after some psychiatric interviews and a lot of waiting around. It is possible he may never be allowed to live in the regular world for the rest of his days.

26

POWELL DESTROYED

Many years before the John Ford mess got started, Peter Moon, Duncan Cameron and myself were poking around Camp Hero one day. We were accompanied by Cori, a lady who lived in the local area. This was during a period when a huge hole had been dug near the transmitter building and a huge detoxification program was supposedly underway. Although a clean up of toxic materials was underway, I believe this was also used as a ruse for other operations. The place is still loaded with toxicity.

As the four of us drove around in Peter's car, we noticed that the front gate to Camp Hero was opened. After seeing a car go right through, we drove around the neighborhood right next to the base before parking near a grass field where we could monitor any traffic coming in and out of the base. Soon after we parked, a huge dump truck full of what looked like debris came out of the base. To our surprise, there was no license plate on the rear. This is illegal, so we thought there might be something very fishy. We took off and pursued the truck all the way from Montauk Point to the village of Montauk. The truck moved at a pretty good clip, and we wondered if he was trying to evade us. It is about seven miles between Montauk Point and the village, and as there are no other roads to speak of, there was really no reason for the driver of the truck to think he was being pursued. After he passed through the village at a good clip, we kept on his tail. As soon as he got out onto the main highway, he obviously sensed we were following him. He sped off at a tremendous rate and was flying along at well over seventy miles per hour. Peter had to stay just above seventy to even keep him in a reasonable distance, but the truck was going faster. Believe me, a big dump truck going that fast looks very suspicious, particularly in a rural area like Montauk. We followed him another seven miles or so to Amagansett where he was forced to slow down to a slow crawl. There, we were able to catch up with him and keep pace until we reached East Hampton. This was about a half hour in total. Although it was rather late in the day, we wanted to follow him and find out where he was going with all of the garbage from Camp Hero. Obviously, he did not want us to know. Unfortunately, our friend Cori had to work the next morning and was not up for the trip. We knew it would be a long one. At East Hampton, Peter pulled in front of the truck and saw that it actually had a New York license plate on the front, but only on the front. Although the truck's owners were flaunting the law, we knew it was at least a registered vehicle. We returned to take Cori home and abandoned the investigation. The truck had already passed the East Hampton dump, so we knew it was not going there. We could only assume it was going to Brookhaven in order to dump whatever was in the truck. This adventure remained an enigma in our minds for many years. That was until, one day, the wheels of justice turned and the wind began to blow in a different direction.

POWELL DESTROYED

In November 1998, John Powell, the target of the alleged toothpaste plot by John Ford, was arrested, handcuffed, and jailed on charges he received payoffs for allowing illegal dumping in the Brookhaven town landfill. He was also accused of directing a massive "chop-shop" operation. The shocking news of Powell's arrest was immediately broadcast loud and clear by the New York city media and was said to rock Long Island politics to its very core. None of the news reports we heard included even a scant mention of John Ford or his situation. Nevertheless, floods of coverage by the press painted a very dark portrait of Powell, John Ford's chief nemesis.

Powell was among nineteen people charged in a federal complaint stating they were part of interlocking criminal schemes that included "chop-shops," extortion, as well as arson, obstruction of justice, and the sale of narcotics. In the court documents, he was accused of abusing his political power.

The arrest of Powell, as I have already indicated, was part of a federal sting operation. Local authorities were bypassed, partly because it was feared that certain officials would have compromised the investigation because of their affiliation with Powell. The feds had been watching the chop-shop operation for over a year but did not suspect Powell was involved until they raided a trucking company owned by Joseph Provenzano. The feds had already wired guilty operator/employees who silently cooperated with the authorities. It was into this environment that Powell unwittingly walked and began saying the most incriminating comments possible. He joked to Provenzano that the latter was suffering from the effort to turn "legit" because of wariness about investigators. Powell is quoted in *Newsday* from the tapes saying, "You're not robbing and ____(expletive omitted)____ stealing. It's like the withdrawals from a _____ alcoholic."

The next morning the jokes stopped when federal agents raided Provenzano's salvage yard. Provenzano called Powell, whose tape recorded response was "Some mother_____ pointed them (the agents) your way."

Powell then had the unmitigated nerve to show up at the truck yard and began berating the investigators for harassing him and his brother (who owns a trucking concern implicated in the scheme). He even threatened a detective that "he'd get his gold shield for this."

All of this was extremely brazen behavior for a man who is not even in public office. His power was obviously enormous. The newspapers reported his affiliation with Governor George Pataki and how Powell got him elected. Although Pataki was quick to sympathize with Powell after John Ford's arrest, the Governor was not making quotes on this day.

The chop-shop operation came as an unexpected boon to the feds. When politicians are arrested, it is not usually for something so crass as street crime. Powell had broken some new ground in this regard. Still, the illegal dumping charges loomed even larger for him because they carry heavier penalties. Powell was accused of taking at least $20,000 in kickbacks to allow illegal dumping in the Brookhaven landfill. These allegations were made by the owner of a hauling company who cooperated with the feds. The hauler said he made payments to Lapienski, the chief deputy commissioner of the Brookhaven landfill. In court documents, Powell was quoted as referring to the town dump as "my landfill."

Unlike John Ford, Powell was given a reasonable bail of $100,000 of which only ten percent had to be put up to a bail bondsman. He was released, proclaiming his innocence and vowing to win this legal battle. Fortunately for John Ford, this was a battle that Powell was not going to win. Powell suffered political disgrace and his career in this regard has been virtually destroyed. Finally, and at long last, there was some relief on the horizon. The pressure on John Ford could let up.

Several months later, Ford's attorney worked out a plea bargain with the District Attorney whereby Ford entered a plea of not-guilty by reason of mental incompetence. In accepting the plea, Judge Gary J. Weber acknowledged that it was impossible to murder someone by such means as radium in their toothpaste and directed that Ford be reevaluated mentally for the purpose of returning him to society. Ford's attorney praised the decision claiming it was "technically an acquittal." In fact, John wanted to stand trial but finally accepted the plea bargain after talking to me. I pointed out that the court had already declared him mentally incompetent, and there was nothing he could do about that. He had nothing to lose by accepting their terms. But, it was only after Powell's arrest and fall from power that Ford was acquitted. Any coincidence here?

Before accepting the plea bargain, District Attorney Catterson elicited the approval of the victims of the alleged toothpaste plot in order to satisfy the judge. By approving of John Ford's acquittal, Powell was likely seeking the favor of his prosecutors, but it was too late. Powell had a nightmarish road in front of him.

On December 2nd, 1999, John Powell was found guilty of extortion by a jury for accepting $20,000 from a local trucker for access to the Brookhaven town landfill. Shock waves went through the court room as dozens of supporters gasped or cried. Outside the court, Powell was indignant and showed no signs of contrition. Questioning the fairness of the trial, he said he did learn one thing: "Innocent people go to jail." The Assistant U.S. Attorney, George Stamboulidis, was humble in winning the case for the prosecution. During the trial, he said that the prosecution had "ripped the lid off...the corruption that was John Powell's Brookhaven."

Powell also faced additional charges on racketeering and for being a known accomplice in the chop-shop ring that "chopped" stolen trucks and resold them for $50,000 each. After a couple of months, he pleaded guilty to this charge and admitted his involvement in accepting bribes. This was apparently an effort on his part to reduce the time he would spend in prison.

Just as this book went to print, Powell was given a light sentence of twenty-seven months and was fined $16,000 for his role in the stolen truck ring. He was ordered to turn himself in to federal authorities on June 5, 2000. The $16,000 was restitution for his victims, one of them a lady whose letter was read by the court at the sentencing. She said that it would take years for her family business, founded in 1912, to recover from the loss of two trucks and a bulldozer. There was no mention of any restitution for John Ford and his difficulties.

Powell's attorney indicated an appeal was unlikely.

CHAPTER TWENTY-SEVEN

27

CONSIDERATIONS

Powell's arrest ended a major chapter in Long Island politics and, at first glimpse, seemed to considerably ease the pressure on John Ford. They only problem is that, at this writing, John Ford has been returned to the sanitarium, and there is no imminent expectation for his release. He has definitely received a considerable amount of drugs, if only for his back condition. His UFO investigations have been rendered null and void. If he is released, there is always the possibility that he might renew them. Even if he is discredited by reason of the court declaration, he could always pass data on to others who could release it under a more suitable public relations image.

I do not really know if John Ford was arrested for his UFO research, but there are ample questions that need answering in regard to this. One thing is very certain. John Ford had made himself the number one enemy of John Powell by reason of his investigations and knowledge of the town dump. There was also plenty of infighting between the two with regard to Brookhaven politics. It is obvious that the entire affairs between the two men were multilayered and extend to regions that we may never find out for sure. To his own detriment, John Ford was a master at compartmentalizing information and keeping things secret. He shared a lot with me, but I know there was plenty he did not share. I certainly do not tell everything I know. When one's survival is threatened, one has to be very discerning who they exchange information with. If he had shared more of his information with other people, maybe he would not have ended up so alone and betrayed by the people he thought were supporting him.

In this book, we have kept speculation to a minimum by sticking to the newspaper accounts and actual facts of the case with regard to John Ford and John Powell. To say that Powell was part of a UFO cover-up is going a bit too far if one expects incontrovertible documented proof. However, we do have a thread which ties Powell to Camp Hero and that is the dumping fiasco. Was it just a coincidence that Duncan, Peter, and myself happened to be at Camp Hero the day that truck made its run? After all, Montauk is not a place any of us visit very often and usually not all together. It remained a mystery for years.

According to what I heard, the toxic waste at Camp Hero was disposed of by Grimes, a major contracting company at Montauk who does most of the work at Camp Hero. I was told that Mr. Grimes is a cousin of Lapienski, the chief deputy commissioner of the Brookhaven landfill. Allegedly, some funny deal was worked out between these characters. Even if this is true, it still leaves a major smoking gun.

One of our astute readers of the *Montauk Pulse* pointed out that the government has plenty of outlets where nuclear waste can be dumped. Further, these landfills require that all nuclear waste be identified with regard to where it came from as well as an explanation as to when and how it was produced.

Next, we have to consider who has ultimate responsibility for the disposal of such waste with regard to Camp Hero. It is the Army Corps of Engineers. According to what I heard, they contracted Grimes and looked the other way. Of course, they might not be aware of what happened. But, if so, why would they do such a thing? Is it because they did not want to be bothered? Remember, the government has facilities for such dumping. As the contractor is being paid, how much extra money is he really going to save by going to Brookhaven? Whatever it might be, it is certainly not worth the risk of being caught. The penalties are too severe. The Army Corps of Engineers is responsible for the clean-up as it is a former military facility. There is no dispute about this. Keep in mind that Camp Hero is still a very top secret "hot" area. All of the books about Camp Hero at the Montauk library were taken off the shelves in the 1990's as they were considered confidential by the military. It is obvious that whatever was being transported out of Camp Hero for dumping did not meet the criteria for being dumped in a government fill. Someone in the military wanted Grimes or whoever to dump it in a clandestine matter. Exactly how complicit local politicians such as Powell were in this scheme is anyone's guess. How deep the connections run is another question, but it is obviously the tip of an iceberg.

The *Montauk Pulse* reader who pointed out the availability of government landfills also had something else interesting to say. He said he read in a magazine where Bob Lazar, the refugee scientist from Area 51, explained how one particular UFO's propulsion system worked. Inside the power propulsion compartment of this

UFO was a lead-metal cup which contained element 114 (also its atomic number). Underneath the cup, the element is bombarded with protons which raises the atomic number to 115 whereupon the element becomes element 115. This newly produced element decays in a few seconds. Secret research from the atomic bomb tests during World War II revealed that decaying atoms also give off gravity waves. This particular UFO used an amplifier similar to a radio amplifier in order to harness gravity. These amplifiers are housed in three metal balls underneath the craft which enable the gravity waves to surround the ship and thereby defy gravity. Obviously, all of this produces radioactive waste which cannot be easily accounted for. Whatever waste matter was at Camp Hero and exactly what it was used for is anyone's guess.

At this point, I can only make conclusions based upon the data thus far uncovered. I do not know everything. We do know that after John Powell was arrested, *Newsday* reported that police commissioner Cosgrove was fired because the feds wanted to have a more cooperative commissioner in there in order to assist with the investigation of Powell. My friend, the Colonel, believes that I was the main target in the apprehension of John Ford. They apparently believed that without me, John Ford could not do too much.

It is believed that the group who was after me and John Ford is called Omega. One of their main connections in Suffolk County is supposed to be through the mob. The Kennedy family are also reported to be associated with the Omega order. This could perhaps explain the downing of JFK Jr.'s plane on the anniversary of Flight 800. Someone could have been sending a message. The navy was very active in the recovery of the bodies. The autopsy was

CONSIDERATIONS

accomplished in record time and all the wiring in the plane was completely fried and nonfunctional. Only an electromagnetic pulse like a particle beam could have done damage like that. Brookhaven also publicly reported that their particle accelerator was turned on the day of that tragic incident. These are questions that will certainly not be broached or fairly considered in the mainstream press. Instead, there will be "tunnel vision" investigation.

John Kennedy Jr. was in the middle of a lot of controversy before he died. The regular press had him talking with a Mossad agent the day he crashed. Kennedy wanted to report on certain conspiracies and assassinations in Israel, but the agent warned him off. Kennedy also had my book *The Montauk Project* placed in his hands according to a friend of mine. Although he lived right next to Camp Hero during summer months as a teenager, he never acted on this line of investigation. After his death, *Life* magazine featured a cover photo of Kennedy at Montauk when he was a teenager. The photo was taken by Peter Beard, a photographer who lives next to Camp Hero.

Although exactly what happened with Kennedy is unknown, it is known that there are many factions within the U.S. military and U.S. Government. One hand does not always agree with the other, and there is a lot of infighting. Between Kennedy, Powell, and the illegal dumping, one thing is clear. All roads seem to lead back to Montauk.

THE MUSIC OF TIME

28

THE FUTURE

If I was the main target of John Ford's adversaries, it might have had to do with something more than the illegal dumping that was taking place. While the legal fiasco between Ford and Powell unfolded, I was still wheeling and dealing as a result of my radio deals. I ended up setting up a real estate trust where I controlled all of the property deeds but did not have to pay capital gains along the way. Liquid assets began to accumulate at a rapid rate because the rent checks were pouring in. If some accounting maneuver was not done soon, there would have been a tremendous tax consequence. So, my sharpie financial lawyer said that I ought to put my money overseas. We chose Banco Nacionale in Barbados because that was where the CIA had their slush funds. We figured if it was good enough for them, it was good enough for me. I also knew that the Air Force kept accounts in this bank, too. Everything was arranged through legal corporations, accounting, and the like. I left this in the hands of my lawyer.

Money went back and forth between the bank and my holdings in the states. I had bought my way into WONG and WDAC up in Hartford. I was also doing some remodeling work on my fifty acres in Cape Cod. What had once been millions had dwindled down to about half its original value. Needing about $100,000 for a transaction, my lawyer sent down a man to do the arbitrage necessary to release the money. The arrangements were not as simple as just requesting a wire transfer. All of a sudden, the accounts were frozen in Barbados. If you remember, there was a huge financial disaster in January of 1999 that hit most of the Oriental banks. Banco Nacionale, it turned out, was tied to the Oriental banks through its ownership. We were told that we could take out $10,000 in local currency, but that was it. This was not near enough, and we complained. Soon after our complaint, we received a letter from the bank that indicated that if I signed a certain document, I would be guaranteed one third of the assets originally deposited. My lawyer advised me against this because if I did sign it, I would end up with only a little bit over a million dollars. If we waited until everything smoothed over, I would probably get the original four million.

My connections to the Air Force turned out to be quite helpful. They knew I was in trouble and was about to lose four millions dollars. I was approached by a young Air Force lieutenant who told me that the Air Force was able to take their money out of Banco Nacionale in the form of Military Treasury Notes. These are issued by the U.S. Treasury but are only for military use. The lieutenant suggested that when the Air Force took their money out, I could authorize them to take my money out and put it in the military financial network. So, my money was withdrawn in military treasury notes, but I could not have access to it. We thought I would be able to take it out of the military financial network whenever I needed it. This was not the case. There were too many legal strings

THE FUTURE

attached. I sat with a group of my friends in the Air Force, and we tried to figure out how I could get out of this mess. Someone said I could use the credit to buy a cruise missile or an airplane on the surplus market. This did not appeal to me, so I asked about property. They said that there was plenty of property. I was referred to the Defense Logistics Agency which handles surplus sales. I thought that maybe I could buy one million dollars of surplus and maybe sell it for two million.

A lady we affectionately called "Tank" suggested a missile silo out in Wyoming. I said that I wanted something in New York. Eventually, she sent over a land manager for the northeast region. After going through a catalog with him, I told him that I wanted to buy an old military base, but it had to be wooded and environmentally clean with an accompanying declaration. Hopefully, it would have an underground with some buildings but not too many. That would be too expensive to maintain properly. The land manager made different suggestions. Every place he showed me in the catalog had a map location and a photo of the property. I eventually found one that was just environmentally certified and turned out to be a communications station that was a "satellite" to a nearby larger base. It was roughly 600 acres with the rights to grab federal property around it on federal quitclaims. If I played my cards right, I would be able to grab about fifteen hundred acres in total. He said that they expected it to sell from somewhere around three to four million dollars and that I should submit a bid. I got the property for an undisclosed amount and salvaged the holdings I originally had in Barbados. It had twenty buildings, six of which I removed. There was a huge underground of 400,000 square feet. As I refurbished it,

THE MUSIC OF TIME

the army contacted me and said they wanted to rent part of the property from May of 1999 to May of 2000. Could we work out an arrangement?

The papers I signed said it was rented to the U.S. Army Millennium Management Group. I suspect this had something to do with Y2K. They indicated they would be finished by May 20, 2000. May 5th, the holiday of Cinco de Mayo, featured a planetary lineup of seven planets in the constellation Taurus. Psychics have said that the energy oddities on the planet will shift after that date. This means that the property will not be a "hot spot" anymore. I know it was because the property features "Spook Hill", named so by locals because of spooky things that go on at one particular hill. There have also been television shows which carted their cameras to a nearby mountain so that they could view what was going on down at "Spook Hill." UFO activities and that sort of thing were also reported. I do not want to reveal the exact location so as to avoid people besieging the place. There is important and possibly dangerous work to do there in the future.

Many years ago, Duncan Cameron channeled in the early 1990's that he and I had two important jobs to do. One of these was referred to as the "Freeman Function." We never knew what it meant except that he would get that "the Freeman Function does this or that." Finally, after we got the transmitter set up for B103, I noticed what this was about. Guess where the transmitter for B103 was located? On Freeman Avenue! That turned out to be the Freeman Function. Presently, there is a large radionics broadcaster hooked to the transmitter and that is the Freeman Function. It transmits "good vibes" for the area.

Duncan also read that a big machine would be built near the "Promised Land." I was not sure what this meant, but we knew there was an area near Montauk that was called the Promised Land. It contained warehouse buildings that were labeled a fish hatchery. This did not make any sense, but Duncan indicated we would go to the Promised Land around the year 2003 and build a big machine that will control the Philadelphia/Montauk vortex from the 2003 point.

After buying the surplus army base, I soon discovered that it was right near an area referred to as the "Promised Land." Apparently, Duncan's reading was uncannily accurate. I had purchased the property without even realizing what the local names surrounding the property were. Further, when you go to the Promised Land at the present day, you can sometimes find this big machine fading in and out of existence. First it is there, and then, it is not there. I have since learned that it is actually coming in from out of the future. The exact location of the building is not real easy to find.

After I bought this property in 1998, I remember Duncan was taking a trip to Egypt where he spent some time in the Great Pyramid. That same weekend, which I believe was the summer solstice, I went to a hamfest in New Jersey. It was incredibly hot, and I was riding around in a senior citizen cart. A lot of my friends thought I might be disabled, but I explained to them I was just tired of exhausting myself in the heat. While riding around, this fellow approached me. Asking me who I was, I told him that my name was Preston Nichols. He then told me that he was me from out of the future. Sure, I thought: I can take a joke. He looked at me rather intensely. He was a little thinner and a little grayer, but he looked very similar. We ended up running around together, and he gave me a little widget which he said was from the future. He wanted

THE MUSIC OF TIME

to take me to my property and show me certain things. Going down to the parking lot, we got in this old powder blue Lincoln Continental. I guessed that it must have been from the late 1960's or early 1970's. After driving for quite a while, I began to recognize that I was going through the Promised Land. We turned onto my property and stopped at the gate house. My caretaker did a double-take because he saw two of us sitting in the car. He said that there were strange things going on up the hill today, but he was not going to go up there.

As we drove up the hill, it was as if we suddenly went over a line that went from a beautiful wooded property with an old derelict base to what looked like just trees standing with no foliage. Some sort of defoliation had occurred on the property. As we drove up to the building, I saw it had a nice paint job on it. Walking into the main building, I noticed there was a tremendous mural painted on the theme of time. In the main hall, the wallpaper consisted of more paintings that were hauntingly similar to my mother's art. There was also an elevator which is not there today. Around fifty to seventy people were walking around. As Preston from the future showed me around, I recognized some of the equipment. He took me down in the elevator to a big pyramid that is underneath the property. There were big crystals inside of the pyramid which were hooked up to all sorts of wiring that was connected to the higher level of the underground. From what I can figure out from this experience, we built some sort of time device on this property. Duncan Cameron's reading indicated that every so often, one could see the 2003 installation. In other words, it was built in or for the year 2003. Whenever 2003 influences our present time, it does a flip. The property exchanges 2003 for whatever the present day is. Duncan also told me certain things about the future which I am not at liberty to go into the full details of at this point. I also saw the golden horse on this property. This is the golden horse that was mentioned in *The Montauk Project*, and was found amidst ruins far in the future. Duncan remembers hopping on the horse in 2003 and riding it back to one million or one billion B.C., but I do not remember the exact date. I currently know where the pedestal is for the golden horse. It contains a cutout where a television monitor can be placed. The purpose of this was ostensibly to take control of the Philadelphia/Montauk vortex in order to make it so that the 1943-1983 project never happened. The idea is to clear up some of the negative effects that resulted from the Montauk Project.

I eventually returned to the hamfest where I had left with my future self. It seemed like only two hours had passed when the time I spent in the future was much longer than that. I eventually saw my future self again, but I was much older and am not going to say much more than that for now. One thing that was indicated to me was that it was OK to see my future self if I was invited.

I am fully aware that this book goes from the incredible and bizarre to the mundane and tangible and then back to the bizarre again. This is how my life has been. I have experienced multiple time lines and have seen myself from the future. This potential exists for everyone. I just happen to be a magnet for it. This has to do with the fact that my purpose is to help mankind get through the coming transition of consciousness. We have already experienced tremendous change as a culture since *The Montauk Project* was published eight years ago. There are a lot more changes ahead. I have not figured everything out and have to struggle with all of this from time to time. My next book is planned to be *The Time Travel Primer* which will go into more technical data about time travel as well as trying to unscramble the 2003 project. That information is not ready to be downloaded yet because I have not processed all of the data.

One thing I did not mention yet is the mystery of where the phone call came from that warned me away from John Ford's house the night of the arrest. The call was traced as having come from the base where the Millennium Management group was working. This is the same base I purchased. The only thing was, I had not purchased it at the time of the phone call! The message evidently came from the future. My friends remember the phone call at the time it happened, so it is not as if I made it up. Also, there was the *Northern Exposure* television show which predicted the fate of John Ford. It certainly appears that forces from the future not only conspired to free me from trouble but also to set me up in business so that I can have an impact on the time line. Nevertheless, there are plenty of counter forces around, too. My money is currently locked up by the IRS to the point where I cannot do much of anything. There are many factions within the government. Some try to help and some try to hinder. I was also contacted through the mail by Ed Zabo, the man who was arrested and served time for posession of explosives in connection with John Ford. He was always suspected to be part of the set up of John Ford. We eventually had a phone conversation. He phoned me, and the number was traced to come from the office complex of a fireworks manufacturer who was apparently implicated in the *Northern Exposure* episode as an arms dealer. Consequently, I decided to stay away from Mr.

THE FUTURE

Zabo. Additionally, there has been a major attack on Peter Moon which appears to be a result of his book *The Black Sun* as well as his job of being my ghostwriter. *The Music of Time* is the first book we have been able to produce in years. While it is not prudent to go into the nature of that attack at this time, I have been assisting him and we are hopeful that the future will see us through.

Remember that, in quantum physics, the future, past, and present all exist simultaneously. The links to the past and future exist primarily through the function of consciousness. My adventures would not be considered so incredible and popular if everyone experienced them in a commonplace manner or if everyone was fully conscious like a Buddha or Christ is idealized to be. My "time muscles" just happen to be little more primed than most everyone on this planet. I hope that as you continue to better your understanding of time that you can have some wonderful adventures as you access your own future selves.

THE MUSIC OF TIME

BY PETER MOON

EPILOGUE

In the introduction to this book, I told you that once you had digested all of the information, I would offer some more perspective on the veracity of what Preston has offered us. Before I go into the specific details and stories with regard to verification of Preston's information, it is necessary to make some comments of a general nature with regard to the whole subject matter of this book and how it must be viewed.

We long ago realized that our reading audience more or less embraces about five different categories. First, there are those who interestedly read anything Preston or I have to say and just flow with it and enjoy the idea stream. These people also hold their own power of discernment and do not necessarily accept everything as literal truth. Second are those who wildly embrace everything and do not use any discernment. Third, are technical people who want to learn anything they can about Preston Nichols and how to build exotic technology that might influence the mind or time itself. Fourth are the mildly curious and sceptical who might find too many points of irregularity with their own mind patterns to get anything out of the subject. While they arguably might be throwing the baby out with the bath water, they are also preserving the status quo of their mind patterns. If they can reject the basic tenets of the Montauk Project, they can rest assured that none of this has anything to do with themselves. Fifth are those who must reject the information at all costs. They read just enough to openly and aggressively reject any information in such a manner as to discredit the entire subject. They would tell you that Preston is an absolute lunatic and has nothing of worth to say.

Included in the above are certain hard core scientists as well as others who are very dissatisfied with practically anything offered by Preston Nichols because it is not handed out in a prepackaged form so they can consume it and understand everything there is to understand about time. They think his utterances do not explain anything. Of course, these people are overlooking the fact that the human condition has been such that we are not exactly clued in on all of the inner workings of nature and creation. It is only in such an environment that a series of legends, experiences, and true data could give rise to something so enigmatic, profound, and intangible as the Montauk Project. If professors in universities understood such things and could explain them, there would be no mystery. Unfortunately, too much of the Montauk information is tainted by the chaos and confusion surrounding Preston Nichols. Considering that nature consistently creates through the interplay of order and chaos, we should not be perplexed this.

Personally, I would like it very much if Preston could put out all of his information in a more concise and packaged format. If you heard the original data as it comes to me, you would find that it contains a lot more chaos than appears within the cover of this book. It is not always a simple job to present it in an organized and understandable format. Sometimes, Preston will say something that does not make any sense. It can be downright wrong. Then, you turn around and find some incredibly outrageous idea he has been sounding off about is undeniably true. In this last regard, nothing was more riveting and jolting in my own

EPILOGUE

life than the drama and intrigue which surrounded the arrest and incarceration of John Ford.

John and I met in Preston's house the February prior to his arrest. He wanted to ask me questions about writing a book, and we discussed the possibilities open to him. From talking to him, it was clear that he had a lot of information concerning the political and industrial connections to black operations such as the Montauk Project. These were leads that Preston was not interested in researching for purposes of personal preservation. John was going to give me an outline and sample chapter by May of 1996, but things became very heated in his own personal life. One day, Preston called me and told me there would be no book coming forth from John Ford.

The first time I visited John Ford in jail, I watched him and Preston talk intelligence agency banter the likes of which I had never heard. It was like two "homeys" talking a different language. There was obviously a lot more going on than the rants of an insane and delusional man. Whatever the intelligence connections with John Ford might be, this is a human rights violation that goes off the top of the scale. It is unconscionable that a man is incarcerated without a quick and speedy trial and is tricked into losing his rights.

Prior to writing the first draft of this book, I asked Preston if it would be all right to go into all of the legal and political factors surrounding the problems with John Ford. As John Powell had been arrested, he said there should be no problem. When he read the first draft, he was very happy in that the work completely vindicated him. Unfortunately, the book could not go into print as it was written. His father and the Colonel both feared it could get him killed. Too many names and pertinent information were included. Although much of the information was public knowledge in that it had appeared in newspapers or been disseminated otherwise, the original book connected too many dots. Hence, I was forced to delete a lot of information. None of this changed the principle components of *The Music of Time*. The overall story is basically the same. Although the other information would have added considerably to the sales of this book, it is deemed better to be alive with less money than dead with more.

I cannot tell you if every last thing Preston has told us is true, but I saw his life dramatically change when the Air Force came into it. It was not a joke or an act. Preston's father also witnessed dramatic changes in Preston's life as the drama around John Ford began to unfold.

After what I have said here, I am well aware that some people will still be perplexed about the experiences and testimony of Preston Nichols. There are too many unknown and unexplained factors. Wouldn't it be nice if we could be handed simple to read text books from teachers that explained everything? We could just nod our heads and smile placidly because everything was clear.

The great unknown is loaded with chaos. It is the job of life to create order out of the chaos. If there is too much order and predictability, then things become stagnant. It is then the job of life to introduce a little chaos and make things interesting again. Preston Nichols would be the first to agree that there are elements of utter ridiculousness in some of his studies. That is merely the reflection of the great pool of life itself. When we consider the plight of John Ford, it is obvious that there are more pressing and dramatic concerns that are not very funny at all. Preston's life, despite the bizarre enigmas, is very serious business. It should not be taken lightly.

EPILOGUE

The music aspect of the book also met with personal intrigue and drama in my own life, but that is too detailed to go into. It is not as dramatic as the John Ford scenario. Although I attempted to verify certain instances of Preston's history in the music business, I found that by the very nature of what he was involved in that it would be impossible to meet with full cooperation. Instead, I was in a position where I would likely encounter deliberate deception.

For myself, one of the biggest enigmas described in the pages of this book emerged when I asked Preston a seemingly innocuous question: "Who is the most talented musician you have ever worked with?" There was no hesitation whatsoever.

"Chuck Hamill, no question," he said with complete conviction.

This man is supposed to be the brother of actor Mark Hamill, but I have found no documented historical record of him save for the picture that appears earlier in this book. While this is the typical profile of a government or a "space-time agent," the enigma was further complicated when he told me that Chuck had at least three other well known identities in the music world: Gary Puckett, Peter Knight and Scott McKenzie.

Scott McKenzie is famous for the song *San Francisco* ("All those who come to San Francisco, be sure to wear some flowers in your hair") which made him a one hit wonder. I had seen Scott Mckenzie on television once, but he did not fit the description I knew of Chuck Hamill in any way shape or form. Common information will tell you that Scott McKenzie was an early friend of John Phillips, the founder and primary talent behind the Mamas and the Papas who was also credited with writing *San*

Francisco. Preston has said that names are bought and sold in the music business all the time, and he is positive that Chuck Hamill actually recorded the song, even if Scott McKenzie got credit for it. In his autobiography *Papa John*, John Phillips states that Scott McKenzie had severe substance abuse problems, as did he himself. Phillips claimed to have written *San Francisco* for the Monterey Pop Festival, an event he also sponsored, so that the concert-goers who came would be loving and peaceful. That was an open statement of intended mood control. Phillips also commented that when it came time for Scott to sing his famous song at the festival, he was completely inept and sounded horrible. Therefore, when the documentary on the film for the Monterey Pop Festival was produced, Scott's was the only song that was dubbed over with the original recording. As the song is not an easy one to sing, one has to wonder what really did happen.

As for Gary Puckett, Preston explained to me that while Chuck did the recordings, Gary Puckett and the Union Gap were a touring band that did the road shows. If you look long and hard enough, you can find potentialities where Preston's stories do hold up.

I am absolutely convinced Preston has some sort of connection to the Moody Blues, but his identification of Chuck Hamill as Peter Knight presents a serious problem to the casual researcher. There was a famous conductor from London named Peter Knight who was credited with the orchestration of the Moody Blues album *Days of Future Passed*. This is identifiable as a man who is much older and different from Chuck Hamill; but, as was already mentioned in the text of this book, a "Peter Knight" appeared in *Rolling Stone* magazine describing his problems with intelligence agencies hounding and hassling

EPILOGUE

him. He was running for cover and was underground. This story fits the exact description of the Chuck Hamill we know from Preston and serves to escalate the enigma factor and gives us cause to embrace the idea of one reality crossing over into another one.

For us to accept the above scenarios, we have to accept that there is incredible duplicity occurring on many different levels. Chuck Hamill earns the status of "tempus fudger" as he can apparently see you, but you cannot see him. If such a thing as "space-time agents" do exist, this is how they would interface with us.

Chuck's brother, Mark, is quite an enigma himself. Although extremely talented in many respects, it is highly doubtful he would be very famous at all if not for his role as Luke Skywalker in *Star Wars*. In a *TV Guide* interview, I once read that he claimed no *X-Files* or UFO experiences but that he would like to have them. This is very hard to take when you consider that he appeared on *CBS This Morning* in 1993 when his house was the only one in the neighborhood that did not burn down during huge fires in Malibu. He explained that he did an American Indian ritual that was designed to preserve the house. Is this not an "*X-Files*" experience? This only backs up Preston's statements that the man was deeply involved in the occult and reveals that he is not being fully candid about his life. What is most peculiar is that none of his biographies anywhere mention that he was involved in the music business at all. There is no question that he was involved in the *Ohio Express* and the *1910 Fruitgum Company*. Why is this ignored by his publicists? There has to be a reason he has obscured his past.

When we consider the mind control aspects of drugs and Montauk with regard to Preston's associations with

Phil Spector, the Rolling Stones, and the Beatles, there is ample evidence to suggest a strong, even if fully unexplained, connection. In the book *He's a Rebel*, it is described how Andrew Oldham, a major pill pusher, fights for management of the Rolling Stones and eventually succeeds. When Phil Spector arrives in London, Oldham turns out to be one of the few people Phil Spector can or will listen to. Keep in mind that Spector was considered to be a dictator and listened to very few people at all. Oldham turns on Spector to drugs for the first time while he is in London, and Spector is highly drugged when he meets the Beatles. Spector then flies back to New York with the Beatles on their first trip to New York for their *Ed Sullivan Show* appearance. He famously disembarks from the airplane with the Beatles and begins a long time association with the group. Oldham, in the above role, fits the exact profile of a controller. In mind control lingo, a controller is someone who controls a mind control victim through drugs, hypnotic commands or whatever.

The picture becomes clearer still when we consider Ronnie Spector, Phil's ex-wife, who accuses him of abusing her and locking her up in his mansion as a virtual prisoner. But, the most telling aspect of Phil Spector is when Danny Davis arranges for La Toya Jackson to meet Spector as he feels it is her best chance to spark a singing career for herself. Described in the book *He's a Rebel*, Spector sits down uncomfortably close to La Toya and offers her a key with the words "Bates Motel" inscribed upon it. She did not understand the reference to the movie *Psycho* until later. His behavior was too bizarre to be believed. After being completely sweet and nice for a short period, Spector would leave and return in an abusive and threatening manner. La Toya tried to get out of his

EPILOGUE

clutches for four hours. Spector would go into tirades every fifteen minutes or so, leave, and then come back "each time with a new personality." Sometimes it was vitriolic, entertaining, or up and down. His extremes reveal the same sort of tortured soul described by Ronnie Spector in her book *Be My Baby*.

The above behavior is a clear description of a symptom that is known as multiple personality disorder. In *The Black Sun*, it was described that manipulation of individuals occurs when people are abused severely and new personalities are developed to cope with the trauma, often carrying out the instructions of a programmer. In one of his biographies, it is described that Phil's problems may have begun when he was playing with the Teddy Bears as a young man. On a gig one night, when he was using the lavatory, a patron is said to have brutalized him and urinated on him. While this was a traumatic event in itself, it may have set the stage for or reinforced different programming. Phil Spector's sister was also institutionalized. He was extremely sympathetic with regard to her condition, and some say it was because he could relate so well to it himself.

Phil Spector was also notorious for putting out records by groups when they did not even sing on the record. The Crystals are just one group in point. This backs up Preston's contentions about recordings not being properly credited to the actual artists. You can also find plenty of other examples of that if you do the research.

The Beatles themselves fit into the mind control mix. Much of what you read about them is publicity oriented and steers away from key truths. Lennon himself decried the official biography of the Beatles and was highly critical of the drug debauched orgies put together for them.

THE MUSIC OF TIME

There is an interesting book entitled *The Lives of John Lennon* by Albert Goldman which describes Lennon as an abusive sufferer of multiple personality syndrome. It chronicles bizarre episodes in the musician's life. At one time, Lennon wanted to make a press announcement that he was Jesus Christ. But, what I found most bizarre about Lennon in the above biography was a trip he took with Yoko to Alborg, a Danish town buried deep in snow in an arctic-like environment. Going there with Yoko to see her daughter, they ended up involved with her ex-husband in a mind control cult whose leader, Dr. Don Hamrick, was trying to link up humans to ETs and saw the Beatles as a natural medium to accomplish this. The Lennons stayed in Alborg for three weeks and took plenty of drugs. The book recounts how Lennon's manager, John Brower, visited Lennon during this period and got to meet Dr. Hamrick. Brower described him as six-foot-three with long stringy gray hair, like Baby Huey. He wore shorts and no shirt with "a hole in his back as big as my hand." The spine was showing, and he could see one of his lungs pumping. His flesh was laced with stitches from major surgery Hamrick had in London a month earlier. Although the doctors wanted him to recuperate for a couple of months, he left after one week. Bower described Hamrick as speaking slowly with a sort of German accent. He showed him a scale model of a Buck Rogers city that was floating mysteriously about a foot above the table. He said he had been given an antigravity secret from the space people and was building a city above Brazil in the clouds. The scale model was to illustrate the power of what he could do. Lennon actually championed this man, but there is no elaboration in the book on the exact nature of the little floating city and how it was accomplished.

EPILOGUE

If there are any doubters about John Lennon's mind control connections after reading the above, they should be convinced by examining Mark David Chapman, the man who murdered the famous Beatle. Chapman was loaded with mind control connections, the most notable of which was discovered with him at the murder site. When he killed Lennon, Chapman did not run away. Although he easily could have done so, he clutched a copy of the book *Catcher in the Rye*. John Hinckley, the man who shot Ronald Reagan, was also found to have a copy of *Catcher in the Rye*. In one of his letters, he told Jodie Foster of how he was distraught over Chapman's killing of Lennon. In 1989, there was another publicized murder where the assassin was armed with a copy of *Catcher in the Rye*. The victim this time was celebrity Rebecca Schaeffer, the young star of the television show *My Sister Sam*.

Despite the obvious associations, authorities never did a proper investigation of mind control in the John Lennon murder case. When Chapman was jailed at Ryker's Island, he was given unprecedented contact with the outside. This included all sorts of strange characters that had motives and opportunity to tamper with him. After all of these visitations, Chapman miraculously changed his plea from "not-guilty by reason of insanity" to just plain "guilty." He had an excellent case for being declared insane. There was a twelve board panel of psychiatrists who were dedicated to determining his mental health, but the possibility or potential of mind control was not discussed even once.

The Beatles also thought enough of Aleister Crowley to feature him on their *Sgt. Pepper* album. Ringo Starr, whose substance abuse problems are legendary, recently released a new album entitled *Vertical Man*. Most people would not know it, but this is a direct reference to a passage in Aleister Crowley's book *Magick: Theory and Practice*.

George Harrison was good friends with the leader of the Hare Krishna movement in America who also happened to be the director of a major pharmaceutical company. There was recently an attempt on Harrison's life by a man who emerged from an asylum and stabbed the Beatle in the chest. Although Harrison has reportedly said there is more to it than a simple murder attempt, the press has been very mum on exactly what the full circumstances of the case were. While Paul McCartney might seem to be the "best boy," he was a public advocate of taking LSD. By his own comments, he now appears to feel very guilty of his role in all of that.

My own reading and interviews with people in the music business indicate that the industry is beset with Mafia and drug connections. Performers are indulged and lulled with sex and drugs to the point there they often lose control of their own lives. The Beach Boys' Brian Wilson is just one example. He was under the complete control of a psychiatrist at one point and was not even allowed to see his own family until they sued the psychiatrist. This was a public outrage which has been well covered elsewhere. Brian's brother, Dennis Wilson, was deeply involved with Charles Manson, the man convicted for his involvement in the Tate-LaBianca killings. Some believe that Dennis Wilson's untimely death by drowning had to do with his connection and ultimate rejection of Charles Manson.

Other observers of the music business have expressed curiosity at how organized crime dedicated so much time and attention to a business which was, particularly in the '60's and early '70's, small potatoes in terms of big business. Why so much interest in a relatively small

EPILOGUE

industry? There are obviously control factors through the music which would make control of this industry very important to those interested in mind control.

Besides checking out various books on musicians and the industry, I have met other people who remember Preston from his days at Bell Sound and Buddah Records. I also consulted Preston's father, Bob Nichols, who describes himself as the "doubting Thomas" of the family when it comes to the Montauk Project. When I asked him if he remembered any of Preston's associations with the music industry, he said he could remember only one time. He said he came home to find the Beach Boys in his living room. They were there so that Preston could fix an amplifier. This story was relayed by Preston in the text of this book. Later, I asked Bob if he realized that the only association he remembered just happened to be one that concerned "Wilsons." He was amused by that and knew what I was referring to. For those of you who are not familiar, the name "Wilson" figures heavily with regard to strange name synchronicities in the other Montauk books.

Another time, I asked Bob if he remembered Preston's association with Chubby Checker. He said, "Oh, yeah, I remember him coming over to the house several times."

Bob himself was not involved in Preston's music career nor any of the Montauk experiences. In fact, Preston has kept his father quite shielded as to many of his activities. If he told him too much, it would only have caused his father unnecessary worry. However, this began to change when the John Ford situation came to pass. At this writing, Bob is in his eighties. He never expected to live past seventy, and the main reason he has stuck around is to do what he can to look after Preston. The last few years have been harrowing but very purposeful for him in terms of keeping an eye on the house for strange characters and the like. His observation of the John Ford case and how it affected Preston removed a substantial amount of doubt from the "Doubting Thomas." That does not mean he believes every last story of time travel, but the immediacy and drama of Preston's situation was no longer something to speculate about. It came too close to home.

If the cold hard truth shows itself through Preston's involvement with John Ford, there is no reason to automatically discount the esoteric aspects concerning Preston's history in the music business. It is just as bone chilling.

There are many more mysteries to uncover for Preston and myself. We are currently planning to write another book about time travel which is tentatively titled *The Time Travel Primer*. Preston himself is also anticipating his own participation in the 2003 project. Life will not be boring. Hopefully, it will be pleasant and free from oppression.

Thank you for all your support.

INDEX

A

Jimmy Abbatiello 125–136
Abbey Road 46, 82
acoustical pick up 78
Adolf Hitler Boulevard 16
ADR 102
African drumming 133
After Dialog Recorder 102
Air Force 185, 202
Aiwa 164
Alan Parsons Project 44
Alborg 220
Sgt. Pepper's Lonely Heart's Club Band (album) 44, 45
aliens 14
Alpine Electronics 162
Amadeus 36
Amagansett 190
America 222
Ampex 350 25
amplifiers 78, 163
amplitude 56, 66
Apple Records 32
Army 184
Army Corps of Engineers 197
astrologers 36
Atlantean civilization 149
Atlantic (Records) 131
Atlantic Ocean 148
Atlantis 158
atomic bomb tests 198

B

B103 (radio station) 171–174, 204
Banco Nacionale 201, 202–203
Barbados 201, 202
Barnstable Broadcasting Corporation 170-171
Bates Motel 218
Bayshore (New York) 24, 25
Be My Baby (book) 219
Beach Baby (song)
Beach Boys 33, 80–81, 222-223
Peter Beard 199
Beatles 32-33, 42, 44-45, 90, 92, 218-221
BeeGees 33
Beethoven 77
Beg, Borrow and Steal (song) 37
Bell Notes 24
Bell Sound 33, 38, 42-45, 49, 81, 82, 223
Bell Sound East 33, 42, 71
Bell Sound West 71
Belough Instruments 24
Beneath the Southern Cross (song) 149
Betar 12, 13
Bethpage High School 128
bias 94, 97
Al Bielek 106
Big Girls Don't Cry (song) 26
Bill (first name) 148
biofeedback 164
Biofiss 15, 116, 148, 159, 164
biosonde 159
BJM 107
black helicopters 57
black magic 75
black noise 109
The Black Sun (book) 209, 219
BMG music 144
Humphrey Bogart 38, 42
Neil Bogart 38, 39, 155
Bruce Botnick 71
Boston Pops 140, 144
Boston Symphony Hall 139, 140
Botnick Company 71
human brain 58
Brazil 220
Break My Stride (song) 105
Brentwood, New York 115, 139
Brookhaven 16-17, 47, 49, 75, 92, 94, 190, 197, 199
Brookhaven Laboratories 15-17, 48, 183
Brookhaven town landfill 192-193
Brooklyn 58
John Brower 220

225

brush development corporation sound-mirror 25
bubble gum music 39
Buddah Records 35, 38–42, 99, 105, 155, 209, 223

C

C.I.A. 16
California 71, 80
Cameo 29, 37
Cameo Parkway 27, 29
Ewen Cameron 17
Duncan Cameron
    104, 106, 112, 114, 119, 144, 189, 196, 204-206
Camp Hero 61, 105, 157, 197
Cape Cod 202
Captain and Tenille 81
Carl Carlton 115
Jimmy Carter 104
Bob Carver 163
Casablanca (film) 38
Caswell's Beach 47
Caswell's Pavilion 47
Catcher in the Rye (book) 221
Catholic Church 118
District Attorney Catterson 193
CBS FM 108, 169
CBS Records 31
CD player 158, 162, 164
Celebration of the Lizard (song) 72
celebrity lemmings 105
Mark David Chapman 221
Chubby Checker
    25-27, 29, 31, 223
Chicago 161, 162
Chinese Theatre 103
chip amps 163
choral arrangements 79
Christ 209
Christ Consciousness 54
Christianity 118
CIA 43, 46, 62
Cinco de Mayo 204
(the) Colonel 185, 198, 213

Columbia Radio network 168-169
Columbia Records 31
Mikee Conet 171
Cray 1 computer 114
Creator 144
Crest Records 25
cross-field head 96
cross-field bias 94
cross-head 94
Aleister Crowley 48, 221
(the) Crystals 219
Cub Scouts 23

D

Ed Sullivan Show 218
Danny Davis 218
Day in the Life (song) 81
Days of Future Passed (album)
    44-46, 216
Dayton P. Brown company 85
Defense Logistics Agency 203
Delta-T antenna 121
Delta-T broadcaster 121
Denon 164
Denver 161
Deputy District Attorney, Martin Thompson 177
District Attorney 176, 188
domain 95
(The) Doors 71–74
Dracula 137
Carmen Dragon 81
Daryl Dragon 81
Dream Sleep 104
Dreamscape (film) 104
drumming 69
Allen Dulles 16

E

U.S.S. *Eldridge* 17
E.M.I. 99
E.M.I. Thorn 44, 54
E.T. Company 163
Earthquake (film) 85–88

Earth's forty-year biorhythm 139-145
East Hampton 130, 190
East Hampton chief of police 63
East Islip 23, 26, 29, 147
echo 89–99
echo units 76
Einstein 143
Einstein-Rosen Bridge 148
U.S.S. Eldridge 15, 148
electromagnetic interference 54
electromagnetic spectrum 50
electromagnetic telepathy 49
electromagnetic waves 54
Electronic Musical Industries 54
Electrosound 99
element 114 198
ELF (extremely low frequency) 87
Jack Ellsworth 169
emitter-follower 120
The Empire Strikes Back (film) 103
Encounter in the Pleiades: An Inside Look at UFOs 139
England 43–44, 81
ESP 35, 73
ETs 220
evacuation tit 163
Ernest Evans 27
Everlasting Love (song) 115

F

Farscape 153
Fatima 118
FCC 169
FDA 160
Federal Communications Commission 98
ferograph 25
FET amplifier 163
FG Industries 174
Arthur Fiedler 139-141, 144
Field Effect Transistor 163
Finale 141
The Finale 137
First Wave (tv show) 154

Fisher audio amplifiers 161
Carrie Fisher 105
FM stereo generators 168
Food and Drug Administration 159
The Fool 53
John Ford 20, 174-175, 184, 187, 191, 195-196, 198-199, 201, 208, 213-215, 224
Ford's bail bond 176
Ford's brother and sister 176
Ford's mother 176
Jodie Foster 221
409 (song) 83
Four Seasons (singing group) 26, 31
Fox Studios 80
fractal analysis 66
fractals 96
Freeman Function 204
Freeport 24
frequencies 56–57
Furnace Wells 101
future book 64

G

Reinhard Gehlen 16
Margo Geiger 13
Germans 16
Go Now (song) 45
Goebbels 16
golden horse 207
Golden Oldies 168
Göring 16
government projects 58
Grand Award of Pickering and Company 24
Great Britain 44
Great Pyramid 205
Grumman Aerospace 128
guitar 78
Gurney's 131

227

H

Chuck Hamill   29, 36-37, 39
   43–45, 132, 215-217
Mark Hamill   18, 29, 35, 39-42,
   47, 72, 101, 105-106, 132,
   215, 217
Dr. Don Hamrick   220
Hare Krishna movement   222
Harlem   58
George Harrison   222
Hartford   201
Harvard University   62
Hawaii   106
Justin Hayward   45
heart rate   65, 69
Jimi Hendrix   77
Hendrix's guitar   78
Camp Hero   189, 196, 199
He's a Rebel (book) 218–219
heterodyne   57
John Hinckley   221
Howard the Duck (film)   104
human mind   55
Huntington Shore Theater   86

I

Iesus   118
IH symbol   118, 121
IHS   118
Illinois   119
implants   125
IRS   208
Island Broadcasting Company   171
ITT   113
ITT project at Brentwood, Long
   Island   139
ITT radio transmitting station   115
I've Had It (song)   24

J

La Toya Jackson   218
Mick Jagger   47–48
Japan   162
Jesus   118, 220

JFK Jr.   198
Jigsaw   107
Journal of the Wills   104
Jumping Jack Flash (song)   47
JVC   164

K

Kamasutra   42
Peter Kelly   14
Kennedy family   198
Rodney King   57
Peter Knight   46, 215, 216
Krugerrand   130
kundalini   64

L

Lake Forest, Illinois   119
Lao Tzu   53
Lapienski   192, 196
Las Vegas   132
Latin   118
Timothy Leary   61
John Lennon   81, 220-221
Joe. E. Levine   39
Joey Levine   39
"life beat" of the human being   67
Life magazine   199
Light My Fire (song)   71
limiter   110
Little Buddah   42, 47
live sound   76
The Lives of John Lennon
   (book) 220
London   216, 218
London Festival Orchestra   46
London Philharmonic   43, 45, 46
Long Island   13-14, 30, 35, 82, 99,
   105-106, 115, 139, 147, 150,
   163, 169, 175, 176, 191
Long Island City   162
Long Island Railroad   13
Long Island UFO
   Network   175, 20
Long Island University   35

Los Angeles 33, 103
Lourdes 118
LSD 62, 222
George Lucas 101, 103–106
Lucas Sound 103
Lucy 29
Bela Lugosi 137

M

Mafia 222
Magick: Theory and Practice 222
magnetic field 55
magnetic pick up 78
Makay company 115
Mamas and the Papas 33, 215
Manhasset, New York 24
Manhattan 12-13, 31, 35, 71, 137, 171
Cal Mann 24-25
Charles Manson 222
matter 55
Mr. Mayer 30-31
Joseph Mazzuchelli 175
Paul McCartney 45, 81, 222
Scott McKenzie 42, 215-216
Mecca of rock recording 33, 80
Melotron 82
Memory Motel 48
Memory Motel (song) 48
Memphis 33
metaphysics 35
Mid-Hudson Sanitarium 188
military intelligence 62
Millennium Management group 208
Robert Milligan 139
mind 55
Mind Amplifier 115–123
mind control 14, 89
MK-ULTRA 17
monochord 53
Montauk 14, 17, 19, 48, 61-63, 94, 98, 104-106, 111-123, 132, 138-139, 153, 157, 189, 196, 199, 207, 223

Montauk Boys 98, 148-149, 150
Montauk Chair 113-114
Montauk house band 130
Montauk library 197
Montauk lighthouse 158
Montauk Manor 104
Montauk Pavilion 47
Montauk Point 63, 157, 189
The Montauk Project 14-15, 18, 48, 54, 59, 61-64, 92, 99, 105-106, 109, 110-113, 119, 123, 128, 138, 139, 141, 159, 167-168, 170, 199, 207, 211, 213
The Montauk Project: Experiments in Time 15, 17, 114, 139
The Montauk Pulse 159, 196-197
Montauk Revisited 163
The Montauk Tour (video) 62
The Moody Blues 44–46, 53, 82, 216
Peter Moon 43, 63, 106, 116, 159, 168, 177, 189, 196, 209
Richard Mohr 150-151
Morgan 130
Jim Morrison 33, 71-75
Mozart 36, 77
murder plot 177
My Sister Sam (tv show) 221

N

In Search of the Lost Chord (album) 53
National Security Act 16
Navy 15
Nazi intelligence 17
Nazis 14, 16-17
NBC 31, 147
nerve pulse 66
nervous system 66–69
neural-net 68, 115
neural-net activity 68
neural-network 69
neurons 67
New Age 69

New Jersey   26, 63, 205
New York   44, 57-58, 80, 131, 161, 176, 203, 218
New York City   24, 43, 168
New York radio   170
Newsday   191, 198
Bob Nichols   18, 214, 223–224
Ginny Nichols   30, 77, 137
Preston Nichols   11, 17, 19, 31, 155, 205, 211-213, 219, 224
1910 Fruitgum Company   39–42, 217
Northern Exposure (tv show) 208
Nostradamus   154

O

occult   35, 47
Ohio   35
Ohio Express   35, 37, 39, 217
ohm   53, 54
Old Universe   104
Andrew Oldham   218
om   53-54
Omega order   198
one-bit converter   163
Yoko Ono   220
orgasmic channels   65
orgasmic cycle   65
Oscar's Bowling Alley   23

P

Paramus, New Jersey   73
paraphysics   98
Parkway Records   29
Alan Parsons   45
particle accelerator   48
particle light   55
Governor George Pataki   192
Patty   169–172
peak limiting   91
phase   56, 58, 65
phase and time differentials   80
Philadelphia   24
Philadelphia Experiment   14-16, 49, 99, 114, 139, 145

Philadelphia/Montauk vortex   205, 207
John Phillips   215
Pickering and Company   24
Plantation Records   42
Pleiadians   139
Plum Island   125
Poltergeist: The Legacy (film) 154
Port Jefferson, New York   173
John Powell   176-177, 191, 195–196, 198-199, 201, 213
Elvis Presley   91
Promised Land   205, 206
Joseph Provenzano   191
psychic energy   63
psychic input   50
psychic overlay(s)   92–95, 97, 102
Psycho (film)   218
Gary Puckett and the Union Gap   42, 216
Gary Puckett   42, 215-216
pulse position   66–69
pyramids   157
Pyramids of Montauk   157

Q

Qabala   53
Quayle, Dan   130

R

R2R ladder D to A converter   163
radionics   121–122, 159
radium   176
RCA   90-91, 140-141, 144, 150
Ronald Reagan   221
The Recorders   23-24
Republican party in Suffolk County   176
Riders on the Storm (song)   82
Riker/Maxson Audio Visual Services Corporation   168-169
John Roberts Estate   149
Rock On: The Illustrated Encyclopedia of Rock N'Roll   39
Richard Rogers   147, 151

Rolling Stone (magazine) 46, 216
Rolling Stones 33, 47, 218
John Rouse 178
Ryker's Island 221

S

San Francisco 215
satanism 48
scalar wave 94, 97
The Scene 138, 141
Rebecca Schaeffer 221
Sci Fi Channel 153
sculpt 76, 90
search warrant 177
Sensuround 86
sex, drugs and rock 'n roll 61–69, 77
sexual energy 63-64
sexual magick 47, 64-65, 72
Sgt. Pepper (album) 44-45, 221
shake table 85
Shannon (song) 112
(electromagnetic) signature 56
Paul Simon 105
6L6 vacuum tubes 75
6688 vacuum tubes 121
6V6 vacuum tubes 78
Skull and Cross Bones society 43
Sky High (song) 107-112
Luke Skywalker 217
Sliders (tv show) 153
San Francisco (Be Sure to Wear Some Flowers in Your Hair) 215
Simon Says 39
sound effects 76
sound waves 50
South America 149
South Haven park 184
South Haven Park crash 183
Southern Cross 149
Southern Cross Project 150-151
Space-Time Labs 159-160
special effects 75, 77–83
Phil Spector 31-33, 35, 44-45, 90, 93, 218, 219

Ronnie Spector 218
spinal channel 65
Spook Hill 204
Spreader of the Mind's Eye (film) 103
St. Mary's Church in East Islip 23, 26, 31, 169
Assistant U.S. Attorney, George Stamboulidis 194
Star Wars (film) 101–106, 217
Ringo Starr 221
stochastic positioning 67
Stony Brook University 30
Stove Pipe Creek 101
Street Fighting Man (song) 48
Studio A 32, 37
subliminals 75, 92–99, 97
Suffolk Community College 30, 35
Suffolk County 198
Suffolk County police 175
Suffolk County Republican Party 177
Summer of Love 42
Super Pro 149
superstring 143
surface barrier transistor 163
Surfin' Safari 48
Swan Lake 122, 137–145
Sympathy for the Devil (song) 48
synch pulse 66–68

T

Tate-LaBianca killings 222
Peter Ilyich Tchaikovsky 77, 137-138, 141, 144-145
Tchaikovsky Swan Lake matrix 144
Teddy Bears 219
The Ten Commandments 39
International Tesla Society 161
Deputy District Attorney, Martin Thompson 177
thought forms 57-58, 65, 122, 123
THX Sound 103

231

time   135–136
time manifold   143
time mark   112
Time Records   24
time sea   143
time travel   46, 123, 138, 148-149
The Time Travel Primer   208, 224
time travel project   150
Time-Life   108
Touch Me (song)   72
tribal rituals   69
truth serums   62
tube chips   163
TV Guide   217
3-D sound   162, 164
20th Century Fox   80
2003 project   224
The Twist (song)   25, 50

U

U.S. Army Millennium Management Group   204
U.S. Treasury   202
U.S.S. Eldridge   17
UFO activities   204
UFO cover-up   196
UFO crash   183
UFOs   175-176, 187
UFO's propulsion system   197
ultrasonic scanning   157

V

vacuum   55
vacuum tit   163
vacuum tube amplifiers   163
vacuum tube era   75
vacuum tube technology   82
vacuum tubes   75, 163
Frank Valenti   26
Frankie Valli   26
The Ventures   26
Vertical Man (album)   221
vibes   56

Victory at Sea   147
Victrola Series   144
Viewlex   99
Voltec speakers   161
Voltex 604   114
Voyager   112

W

WALK radio   169
Wall of Sound   32
Warner Brothers   108
wave light   55
WBZO   170
WCBS FM 101.1.   168
WDAC   201
weather control   65
Judge Gary J. Weber   193
Webelo scouts   23-24
H.G. Wells   145
Westchester   31
Western Electric   32
White Christmas (song)   26
white noise   68, 109–111, 116, 119, 122
Charlie Whitehouse   127
Matthew Wilder   105
Woodrow Wilson   32
Brian Wilson   80, 222
Wilson Brothers   145
Carl Wilson   80
Dennis Wilson   80, 222
Preston B. Wilson   145
Wilsons   223
Winchester Cathedral (song)   82
witness   160
WONG   201
World War II   147, 150, 198
Wyoming   203

X

X-Files (TV show)   217

Y

Yale University   43

Yaphank   183
*You Don't Always Get What You
    Want* (song)   47-48

Z

Ed Zabo   208
Zuma Beach   106

THE BIGGEST SECRET EVER TOLD

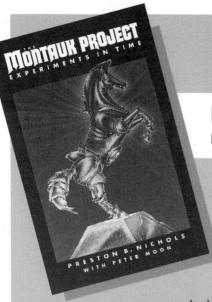

The Montauk Project: Experiments In Time chronicles the most amazing and secretive research project in recorded history. Starting with the "Philadelphia Experiment" of 1943, the Office of Naval research employed Albert Einstein's Unified Field Theory in an attempt to make the *USS Eldridge*, a destroyer escort, invisible to radar. The *Eldridge* not only became invisible on radar screens — it disappeared from time and space as we know it with full scale teleportation of the ship and crew. "The Philadelphia Experiment" was a total disaster to the crew members aboard the *Eldridge*. Psychological disorders, physical trauma and even deaths were reported as a result of the experiment.

Forty years of massive research continued culminating in even more bizarre experiments that took place at Montauk Point, New York that actually tapped the powers of creation and manipulated time itself. *The Montauk Project* is a first hand account by Preston Nichols, a technician who worked on the project. He has survived threats and attempts to brainwash his memory of what occurred. A fascinating account of the research, including the technological applications of changing time itself are given for the first time, along with Preston's intriguing personal story.

■ ■ ■ ■

160 pages, illustrations, photos and diagrams......$15.95

THE ASTONISHING
SEQUEL...

Montauk Revisited: Adventures in Synchronicity pursues the mysteries of time so intriguingly brought to light in *The Montauk Project: Experiments in Time*. *Montauk Revisited* unmasks the occult forces that were behind the science and technology used in the *Montauk Project*. An ornate tapestry is revealed which interweaves the mysterious associations of the Cameron clan with the genesis of American rocketry and the magick of Aleister Crowley, Jack Parsons and L. Ron Hubbard. Also included is the bizarre history of the electronic transistor and how it was developed by the E.T. Company, an apparent front for aliens.

Montauk Revisited carries forward with the Montauk investigation as Preston Nichols opens the door to Peter Moon and unleashes a host of incredible characters and new information. A startling scenario is depicted that reaches far beyond the scope of the first book.

The Montauk Project opened up the mystery of all mysteries. This sequel accelerates the pursuit.

■ ■ ■ ■

249 pages, illustrations, photos and diagrams......$19.95

THE ULTIMATE PROOF

*P*yramids of Montauk: Explorations In Consciousness unveils the mysteries of Montauk Point and its select location for pyramids and time travel experimentation. An astonishing sequel to the *Montauk Project* and *Montauk Revisited*, this chapter of the legend awakens the consciousness of humanity to its ancient history and origins through the discovery of pyramids at Montauk. Their placement on sacred Native American ground opens the door to an unprecedented investigation of the mystery schools of Earth and their connection to Egypt, Atlantis, Mars and the star Sirius.

Preston Nichols continues to fascinate with an update on covert operations at Montauk Point that includes the discovery of a nuclear particle accelerator on the Montauk Base and the development of new psychotronic weapons.

Pyramids of Montauk propels us far beyond the adventures of the first two books and stirs the quest for future reality and the end of time as we know it.

▲ ▲ ▲ ▲ ▲

256 pages, illustrations, photos and diagrams......$19.95

MONTAUK'S
NAZI CONNECTION

*I*n this spectacular addition to the Montauk series, *The Black Sun* continues the intriguing revelations readers have come to expect from Peter Moon as he digs deeper than ever before into the mysterious synchronicities that have made his work so popular.

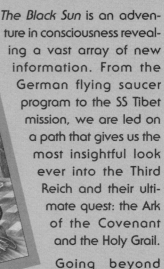

The Black Sun is an adventure in consciousness revealing a vast array of new information. From the German flying saucer program to the SS Tibet mission, we are led on a path that gives us the most insightful look ever into the Third Reich and their ultimate quest: the Ark of the Covenant and the Holy Grail.

Going beyond *The Spear of Destiny* and other attempts to unlock the mysterious occultism of the Nazis, Peter Moon peers into the lab of the ancient alchemists and their white powdered gold in order to explain the secret meaning behind the Egyptian and Tibetan "Books of the Dead".

• • • •

295 pages, illustrations, photos............................$19.95

Journey to the stars—

with Preston Nichols
& Peter Moon's

ENCOUNTER IN THE PLEIADES: AN INSIDE LOOK AT UFOS

★

*T*his is the incredible story of a man who found himself taken to the Pleiades where he was given a scientific education far beyond the horizons of anything taught in universities. For the first time, the personal history of Preston Nichols is revealed along with an avalanche of amazing information the world has not yet heard. A new look at Einstein and the history of physics gives unprecedented insight into the technology of flying saucers and their accompanying phenomena. Never before has the complex subject of UFOs been explained in such a simple language that will be appreciated by the scientist and understood by the layman.

Peter Moon adds further intrigue to the mix by divulging his part in a bizarre project which led him to Preston Nichols and the consequent release of this information. His account of the role of the Pleiades in ancient mythology sheds new light on the current predicament of Mankind and offers a path of hope for the future. The truth is revealed. The keys to the Pleiades are in hand and the gateway to the stars is open.   252 pages......$19.95

MONTAUK: THE ALIEN CONNECTION
BY STEWART SWERDLOW
EDITED BY PETER MOON

Montauk: The Alien Connection reveals the most amazing story yet to surface in the area of alien abduction. This is an autobiographical and factual account from Stewart Swerdlow, a gifted mentalist who was born clairvoyant but haunted by strange time-space scenarios.

After suffering alien abductions and government manipulations, Stewart found Preston Nichols and discovered his own role in time travel experiments known as the Montauk Project. After refusing to break his association with Nichols, Stewart was incarcerated by the authorities, but the truth began to reveal itself. Struggling for his life, Stewart used his mental abilities to overcome the negative influences surrounding him and ultimately discovered the highest common denominator in the alien equation — an interdimensional language which communicates to all conscious beings.

Montauk: The Alien Connection is an intriguing new twist to the Montauk saga which elevates the entire subject to a higher octave.

ISBN 0-9631889-8-4, $19.95
Published by Sky Books, Box 769, Westbury, NY 11590

The Healer's Handbook:
A Journey Into Hyperspace
by Stewart Swerdlow

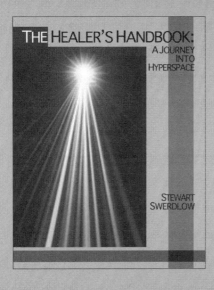

The miraculous and strange become commonplace as you journey out of this dimension with Stewart Swerdlow and discover the Language of Hyperspace, a simple system of geometric and archetypal glyphs enabling us to comprehend universal mysteries ranging from crop circles to the full panorama of occult science. *The Healer's Handbook: A Journey Into Hyperspace* penetrates the secrets of creation through the mysterious principles of DNA, the biological interface between spirit and matter which determines our actual physical characteristics and maladies. Under the guidance of Swerdlow, a gifted mentalist and linguist who has identified the most basic archetypal expressions of consciousness, you will learn that DNA is comprised of four proteins corresponding precisely to universal archetypal symbols which exist in a region of our thoughts identified as Hyperspace. Change the symbols and you change the DNA as well as the physical condition.

The Healer's Handbook: A Journey Into Hyperspace shows you how, and includes a vast panorama of healing techniques and supplementary information including: color healing, dream analysis, numeric values and symbols, auric fields, astral and hyperspace travel, prayer, meditation techniques, and radionics as well as offering exercises designed to unlock DNA sequences programmed within you since the beginning of your existence.

ISBN 0-9631889-9-2, $22.00
Published by Sky Books, Box 769, Westbury, NY 11590

The Montauk Pulse™
A CHRONICLE OF TIME

A newsletter by the name of *The Montauk Pulse* went into print in the winter of 1993 to chronicle the events and discoveries regarding the ongoing investigation of the Montauk Project by Preston Nichols and Peter Moon. It has remained in print and been issued quarterly ever since. With a minimum of six pages and a distinct identity of its own, *The Pulse* will often comment on details and history that do not necessarily find their way into books.

Through 2000, The *Montauk Pulse* has included exciting new breakthroughs on the Montauk story as well as similarly related phenomena like the Philadelphia Experiment or other space-time projects. As of 2000, the scope of *The Pulse* will be expanded to embrace any new phenomena concerning any of the past books on Montauk as well as new developments on the John Ford case and mysteries concerning Brookhaven Labs.

Subscribing to *The Pulse* directly contributes to the efforts of the authors in writing more books and chronicling the effort to understand time and all of its components. We appreciate your support.

For a complimentary listing of
special interdimensional books and videos —
send a self-addressed, stamped #10 envelope to:
Sky Books, Box 769, Westbury, NY 11590-0104

Sky Books ORDER FORM

We wait for ALL checks to clear before shipping. This includes Priority Mail orders. If you want to speed delivery time, please send a U.S. Money Order or use MasterCard or Visa. Those orders will be shipped right away.
Complete this order form and send with payment or credit card information to:
Sky Books, Box 769, Westbury, New York 11590-0104

Name
Address
City
State / Country   Zip
Daytime Phone (In case we have a question) ( )

☐ This is my first order   ☐ I have ordered before   ☐ This is a new address

Method of Payment: ☐ Visa   ☐ MasterCard   ☐ Money Order   ☐ Check

\# ___ — ___ — ___ — ___

Expiration Date   Signature

Title	Qty	Price
The Montauk Project: Experiments In Time..................$15.95		
Montauk Revisited: Adventures In Synchronicity $19.95		
Pyramids of Montauk: Explorations in Consciousness......$19.95		
Encounter In The Pleiades: An Inside Look At UFOs $19.95		
The Black Sun: Montauk's Nazi-Tibetan Connection........$19.95		
Montauk: The Alien Connection................................$19.95		
The Healer's Handbook: A Journey Into Hyperspace.......$22.00		
The Music of Time..$19.95		
The Montauk Pulse (1 year subscription).....................$12.00		
The Montauk Pulse back issues (List at bottom of page.) $3.00 each		
Subtotal		
For delivery in NY add 8.5% tax		
Shipping: see chart on the next page		
U.S. only: Priority Mail		
Total		

Thank you for your order. We appreciate your business.

SHIPPING INFORMATION

United States Shipping

Under $30.00 ....add $3.00
$30.01 — 60.00 ...add $4.00
$60.00 — $100.00 add $6.00
$100.01 and over ..add $8.00

Allow 30 days for delivery. For U.S. only: Priority Mail—add the following to the regular shipping charge: $3.00 for first item, $1.50 for each additional item.

Outside U.S. Shipping

Under $30.00.........add $8.00
$30.01 — 60.00...add $11.00
$60.00—$100.00 add $15.00
100.01 and over...add $20.00

These rates are for SURFACE SHIPPING ONLY. Do not add extra funds for air mail. Due to the vastly different costs for each country, we will not ship by air. Only Visa, Mastercard or checks drawn on a U.S. bank in U.S. funds will be accepted. (Eurochecks or Postal Money Orders can not be accepted.)